THE NATURE NOTEBOOK SERIES

EDITED BY

ANNA BOTSFORD COMSTOC

THE PLANT & FLOWER NOTEBOOK

BY
ANNA BOTSFORD COMSTOCK

ASSISTANT PROFESSOR OF NATURE-STUDY
CORNELL UNIVERSITY

THE COMSTOCK PUBLISHING COMPANY
ITHACA, NEW YORK

THIS EDITION PUBLISHED 2021
BY
LIVING BOOK PRESS IN ASSOCIATION WITH HEARTHROOM PRESS

ORIGINAL WORK PUBLISHED 1915
BY
THE COMSTOCK PUBLISHING COMPANY

FOR MORE INFORMATION, CONTACT:
HEARTHROOM PRESS
INFO@HEARTHROOMPRESS.COM

ISBN: 978-1-922634-39-9

A catalogue record for this
book is available from the
NATIONAL
LIBRARY
OF AUSTRALIA   National Library of Australia

A PLANT is a living being, just as a boy or girl is a living being, only it is different in form and in habits of life. A plant consists of root, stems, leaves, flowers and fruit, and each of these is as necessary to the life of the plant as are arms and legs, eyes, mouth, and stomach to a boy or girl. Before we can understand a plant, we must know just what each of these parts do for it. In order to grow, a plant must have light, water. Food, and air, just as does a boy or girl.

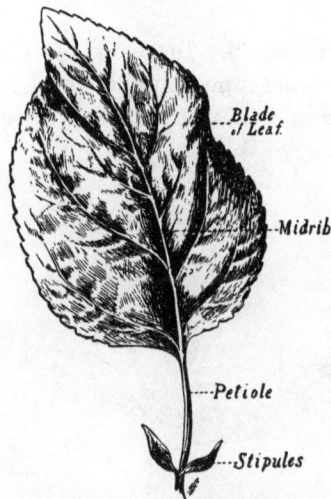

A leaf with parts named.

The Leaf

The leaf makes the food for the plant. The food of plants is largely starch. The leaf is a "starch factory" and it is run by sunshine power. The green pulp in the leaf is the machinery. The raw material is brought up from the roots in the sap, and is also taken from the air. The product is mostly starch. But the growing parts of the plant cannot "eat" starch until it is changed to sugar. So after the leaf makes the starch it has to digest it, i.e. change it to sugar, and then the sap carries it to the growing parts of the plant.

*Leaves used as store-
house for food
for plant.*

The stem or petiole of the leaf is for the purpose of holding the leaf out where it can get the light of the sun so it's machinery can be set in motion. If you place a geranium in the window, the petioles of its leaves will soon bend so each lead can face the light. The midrib and its veins of the leaf form its framework to help keep it spread out in the sunshine. They also carry sap.

Plants breathe somewhat as we do; there are little holes in the surfaces of the leaves and also of the stems to admit the air.

Some leaves are simple like those of the daffodil, violet, and hepatica. Some leaves are compound like those of the rose, clover. A compound leaf is composed of several little leaves or leaflets.

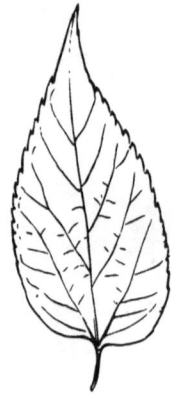

Compound leaf.   *Compound leaf.*   *Simple leaf.*

Leaves may be set upon the stems opposite each other as in the maples, or alternate like the corn or geranium, or they may be attached to the root by their own stems as in the strawberry or hepatica. Sometimes the leaves are used as storehouses for food as in the case of bulbs of lilies, onions, etc.

The Stem and Branches

The stem and branches of the plant are for the purpose of holding the leaves up and out where they can reach the light, and of holding the flowers where they may be seen by insects and the fruits so that they may be scattered. The stem and branches also serve as channels to carry water and dissolved food to the leaves, flowers ,and to all the growing parts of the plant. Stems are also storehouses for food. The thick stem of the horseshoe geranium is an example. There are also underground stems, that are used as storehouses like those of the potato and the jack-in-the-pulpit, and many others.

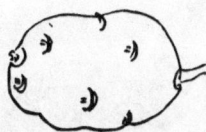

Potato.

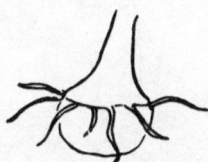

Jack-in-the-Pulpit.

Underground stems used as storehouses for fuel.

Running rootstock, an underground stem.

Twining stem.

The Root

The chief difference between a root and a stem is that he stem grows upward and the root downward. The roots reach out, and through the root hairs on their rootlets take in water and whatever plant food in the soil that is dissolved in the water. The roots also serve to hold the plant in place. The root may be fibrous like the roots of grass and corn, or it may be in the form of a tap root like that of the dandelion. Tap roots contain stored food for the plant. When much food is stored in such roots they are called fleshy. Such are the roots of turnip, carrot, radish, and many others in which is stored the food, which is made one year to be used the next for growth and maturing of seeds.

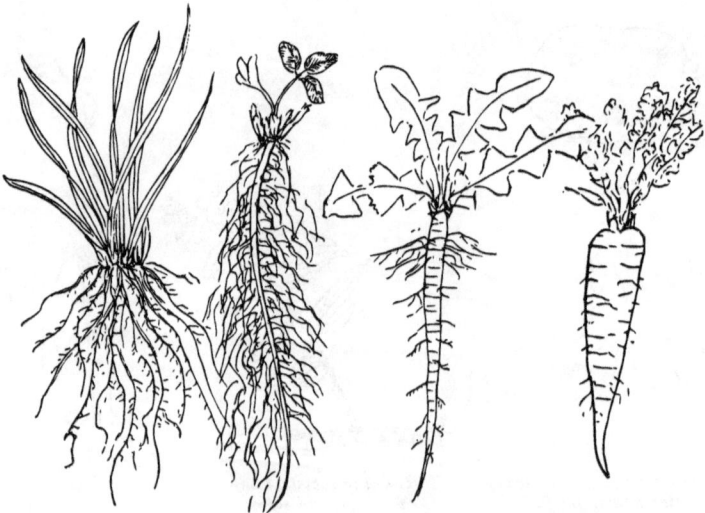

Fibrous roots.   *Tap root.*   *Fleshy root in which much food is stored.*

HOW TO UNDERSTAND A FLOWER

The beautiful part of the flower is the *corolla*, which is made up of divisions called *petals.* The petals are usually white or bright-colored. The bright colors are advertisements to the insects, saying in insect language: "Fly right this way and get some pollen and nectar." The odor of a flower is also an advertisement to the insects telling them where there is pollen and nectar.

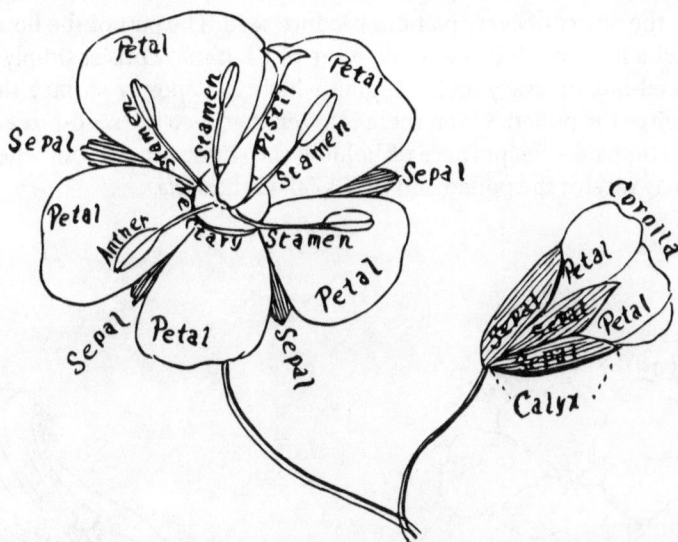

The nectary or 'honey well' of a flower is always placed so that the visiting insects must press against the pollen and stigma in order to reach it. Usually, the nectary is at the very bottom of the flower. Sometimes it is in a special 'well,' as in the nasturtium or violet.

Many times the petals of a flower are united to make a tube- or funnel-shaped flower.

The petals are often not all the same shape as in the sweet pea or pansy, or nasturtium. When they are thus irregular it is for the purpose of forcing the visiting insects to come more surely in contact with pollen or stigmas.

The outside covering of the flower, when in the bud, is called the calyx and it is made up of divisions called sepals. Sometimes the sepals serve to protect the ripening seed as in the pansy. Sometimes the sepals change color and become part of the beautiful blossom as in the tulip and larkspur. Sometimes they form the nectar-well as in the nasturtium. Sometimes the sepals are joined into a small tube as in the petunia. But of whatever form, the office of the sepals or calyx is generally to protect the flower in the bud, and also to protect it if it closes during nights and stormy days.

The most important parts of the flower are not the bright-colored petals or sepals, but consist of the parts which produce the seeds; for it is the object of every plant to produce seed. The part of the flower in which the seeds grow is called the pistil. It may consist simply of a seed-box or ovary and a stigma which is a spongy surface that receives the pollen. Often there is a stem between the seed-box and the stigma for the purpose of holding the stigma up and out where it may receive the pollen and this is called the *style*.

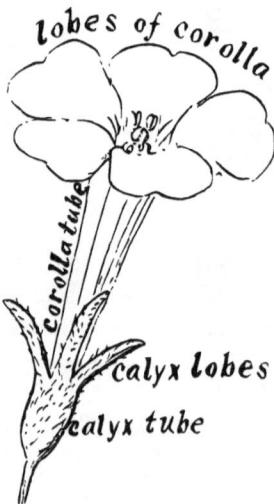

Petunia.

Nasturtium.

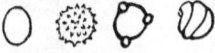

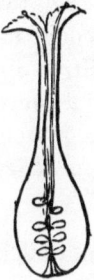

Pollen grains above greatly enlarged. Diagram of a pistil showing two pollen grains on the stigma and the pollen tubes reaching down to the young seeds.

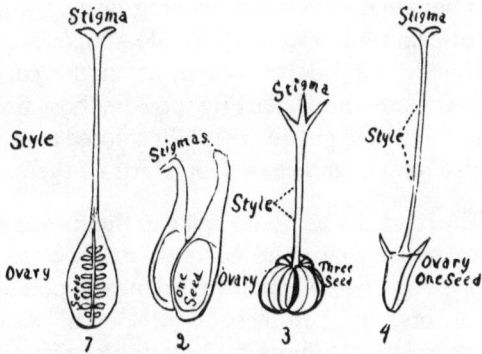

Some different forms of pistils.

The pollen is developed in a little pocket called an anther. This pocket opens when the pollen is ripe and lets the pollen out so that it may be carried by wind or insects to a waiting stigma. Although pollen looks like dust, yet, if we could see the pollen grains under a microscope, we should find them of carious forms and sometimes ornamented. When the pollen grain rests upon the stigma there grows from it a little thread-like tube which finds its way down through the style and the walls of the seed-box until it reaches the young seed or ovule. If one of these ovules is not reached and fertilized by a pollen tube it will never grow into a perfect seed, but will wither and fail to sprout.

Sometimes the anther or pollen-pocket is set close upon another part of the flower, but usually there is a stem to the anther called a filament which serves to hold the pollen-pocket out of up where the pollen may be reached by insects or may be cast out on the air and carried by the wind. An anther and its stem together are called the stamen.

Sometimes the pollen of a flower fertilizes its own seed. But more often the pollen of some other flower does this, -- because by thus having two separate parents the seeds are likely to be more vigorous and stronger. Since the flowers cannot walk or fly to get pollen from other flowers they use other carriers. One carrier is the wind, the other are insects and humming-birds. Since the wind does not care for beautiful flowers, those blossoms which are wind fertilized are usually not bright-colored, as in the corn and pines. But since insects and birds like bright colors those flowers that induce insects to carry their pollen are bright colored to attract the insects and may also have fragrance or odor to attract them.

The rewards the flowers give to the insects for carrying their pollen are pollen to eat and nectar to drink, or to make into honey, if the insect is a bee. More flowers depend upon bees than upon any other carriers. The bumblebees are specially useful in thus befriending the flowers. Humming-birds are also effective pollen carriers.

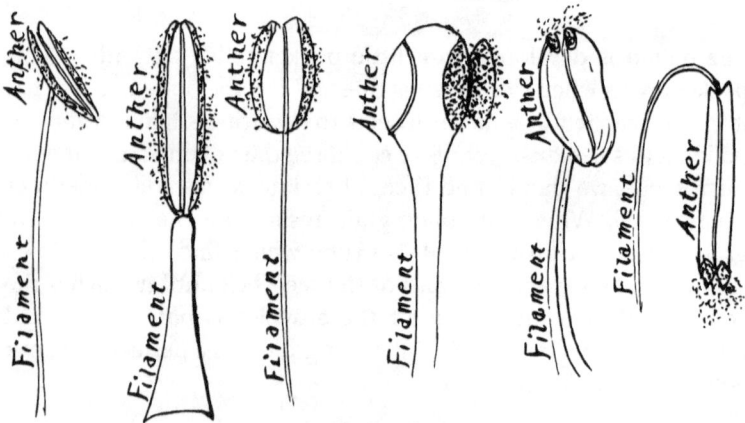

Some different forms of stamens.

Blossoms have various ways of receiving the pollen from their pollen-carriers and avoiding having their seeds fertilized by their own pollen. The most common ways are as follows: 1. To have their own stigmas ripen so as to be ready for pollen either before or after their own pollen is ripe, -- the common garden pink is an instance of this. 2. To have their stigmas so situated that they cannot receive their pollen from the same flower, as in the bluets and primroses. 3. To have the pollen borne in the flower of one plant and the seeds in those of another as in the willows, poplars, pumpkins and cucumbers.

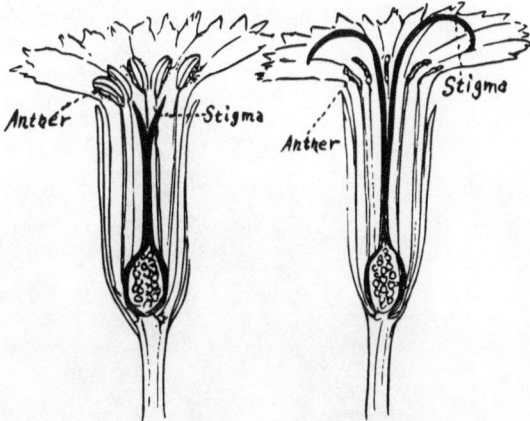

Early stage of garden pink in which the pollen is ripe but the stigma is not.

Later stage of the garden pink in which the pollen is gone and the stigmas are ripe.

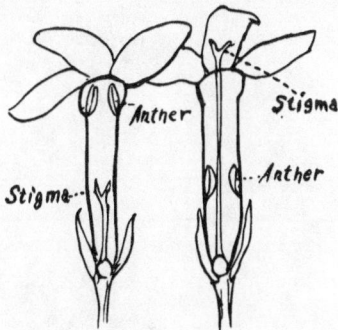

Bluets, which like the primroses, have two forms of flowers with stigmas and anthers arranged so as to secure an exchange of pollen from insect visitors.

INDEX TO PLANT NOTES

INDEX TO PLANT NOTES

UNDERSCORE THE WORDS DESCRIBING THE PLANT.

1. Date

2. Name

3. Where is the plant found? In open field, hill-side, road-side, garden, woodland, swamp, brook-side, shore of pond or stream, in or on water?

4. How high does this plant grow?

5. Is the stem stiff, pliable, straight, drooping, twining, or creeping? Smooth, downy, rough, or thorny?

6. Is there a single stem or many coming from the same root? Is the stem branched? If the plant has a climbing habit, by what means does it cling to its support?

7. If the plant is a weed, or a cultivated plant, or very plentiful, study its roots. But if it is a beautiful wild flower, do not disturb it, as it is wrong thus to spoil our woods. Is the root fibrous or is it a tap root? Is it a storehouse for food?

8. Do you know whether the plant grows every year from the seed -- an annual, or does it live two years --a biannual; or does it grow year after year from the root -- a perennial?

9. Do the leaves grow at the base of the plant or along the stem? If along the stem, are they opposite or alternate? Is the leaf simple or compound?

10. Are the lower leaves of the same size and form as the upper leaves? Are the leaves polished, smooth, downy, hairy, or rough?

11. Sketch or trace a leaf, being careful to show its stem, veins, and especially to represent accurately the edges.

12. Where on the plant are the flowers borne? What is their general color?

13. Does each flower stand by itself or is it in a group with other flowers, if so, are the flowers arranged in a cluster or along the stem?

14. Which flowers blossom first, the nearest to the tip of the stem, or those nearest the base? In the case of the flowers that are in a cluster, do the outside or the center bloom first?

15. Study a single flower. Is its stem short or long, does it arise from the base of the plant or does it branch off of the stem of the plant? If the latter is the case, is there always a leaf where it comes off the stem?

16. Study the calyx or sepals. How many are there? Are they united?

17. Study the bud. Do the sepals protect the flower when it is in the bud? Do they protect the flower if it closes at night or during stormy days to protect its pollen?

18. Do the sepals fall off early as with the poppy, or do they remain after the seeds ripen? Do they protect the ripening seeds?

19. What color are the sepals? Do they always remain the same color or do they change color as with the lilies and tulips?

20. How many petals has the flower? How are they colored?

21. Sketch a single flower showing its sepals and petals, their form and arrangement.

22. Do you find stamens in the flower? If so, how many? Have they filaments or stems? Are they fastened to the petals? Are the filaments united at the bases as the hollyhock or geranium?

23. What is the color of the anthers? Is the anther attached at the middle or end to its stem, or filament? What color is the pollen? Can you see how the anther opens to let the pollen out?

24. Sketch a stamen showing the anther and filament.

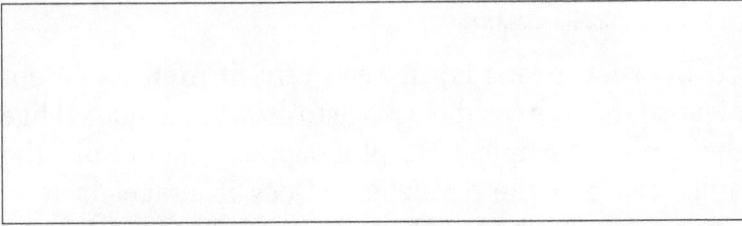

25. At the center of the flower find the pistil. Are there more than one, if so, how many? Is there a stem or style connecting the seed-box with its stigma? Is there more than one stigma for each ovary?

26. Sketch the pistil showing the seed-box or ovary, the stigma, and the style.

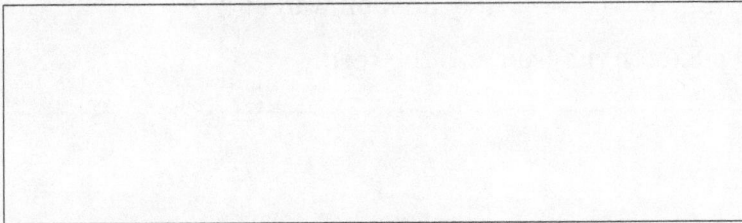

27. Is the blossom fragrant? Is there a nectary in the blossom? Watch the insects that visit the blossom and let them show you where the nectar is hidden.

28. What insects do you find visiting the flowers? Describe how they come into contact with the pollen and stigma, while they are seeking the nectar.

29. Do the flowers close during nights and dark stormy days? If they do not close, do they bend over? How do these movements protect the pollen?

30. How are the ripening seeds protected? Is each seed in a separate husk by itself? Is it with others in the pod-seed box or capsule? Are there many seeds together within one covering?

31. Describe the fruit.

....

....

....

....

....

....

32. By what means is the seed carried from its parent plant so that it may find a place to grow? Is it winged like the elms and maples? Has it a pappus balloon, like the milkweed and the dandelion? Does it attach itself to passers by, like the burs? Are the seeds blown out or are they shaken out by the wind as in the tulips and poppies? Are they thrown out like the seeds of witch hazel or jewelweed? Are They scattered by living creatures, as the squirrels carry acorns and nuts, and the birds berries and wild cherries? Do they float on water?

33. Sketch the fruit and the seed.

34. Is the plant beneficial or of any special importance to us? Is it beautiful? Is it a weed? Is it of use to animals or birds? If so, describe how.

Consult the manuals of plant and flower books and give an account of every thing that is of interest concerning this species, including its native place, its history and its uses by man; and any quotations from literature ---- especially poetry that may have been written concerning this species.

UNDERSCORE THE WORDS DESCRIBING THE PLANT.

1. Date

2. Name

3. Where is the plant found? In open field, hill-side, road-side, garden, woodland, swamp, brook-side, shore of pond or stream, in or on water?

4. How high does this plant grow?

5. Is the stem stiff, pliable, straight, drooping, twining, or creeping? Smooth, downy, rough, or thorny?

6. Is there a single stem or many coming from the same root? Is the stem branched? If the plant has a climbing habit, by what means does it cling to its support?

7. If the plant is a weed, or a cultivated plant, or very plentiful, study its roots. But if it is a beautiful wild flower, do not disturb it, as it is wrong thus to spoil our woods. Is the root fibrous or is it a tap root? Is it a storehouse for food?

8. Do you know whether the plant grows every year from the seed -- an annual, or does it live two years --a biannual; or does it grow year after year from the root -- a perennial?

9. Do the leaves grow at the base of the plant or along the stem? If along the stem, are they opposite or alternate? Is the leaf simple or compound?

10. Are the lower leaves of the same size and form as the upper leaves? Are the leaves polished, smooth, downy, hairy, or rough?

11. Sketch or trace a leaf, being careful to show its stem, veins, and especially to represent accurately the edges.

12. Where on the plant are the flowers borne? What is their general color?

13. Does each flower stand by itself or is it in a group with other flowers, if so, are the flowers arranged in a cluster or along the stem?

14. Which flowers blossom first, the nearest to the tip of the stem, or those nearest the base? In the case of the flowers that are in a cluster, do the outside or the center bloom first?

15. Study a single flower. Is its stem short or long, does it arise from the base of the plant or does it branch off of the stem of the plant? If the latter is the case, is there always a leaf where it comes off the stem?

16. Study the calyx or sepals. How many are there? Are they united?

17. Study the bud. Do the sepals protect the flower when it is in the bud? Do they protect the flower if it closes at night or during stormy days to protect its pollen?

18. Do the sepals fall off early as with the poppy, or do they remain after the seeds ripen? Do they protect the ripening seeds?

19. What color are the sepals? Do they always remain the same color or do they change color as with the lilies and tulips?

20. How many petals has the flower? How are they colored?

21. Sketch a single flower showing its sepals and petals, their form and arrangement.

22. Do you find stamens in the flower? If so, how many? Have they filaments or stems? Are they fastened to the petals? Are the filaments united at the bases as the hollyhock or geranium?

23. What is the color of the anthers? Is the anther attached at the middle or end to its stem, or filament? What color is the pollen? Can you see how the anther opens to let the pollen out?

24. Sketch a stamen showing the anther and filament.

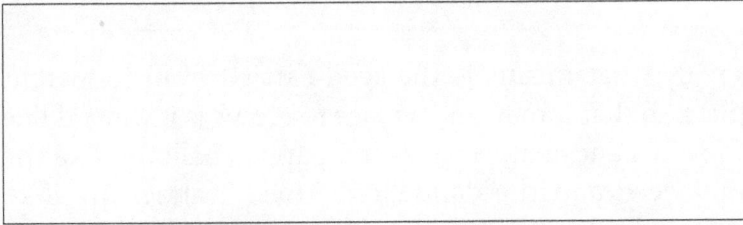

25. At the center of the flower find the pistil. Are there more than one, if so, how many? Is there a stem or style connecting the seed-box with its stigma? Is there more than one stigma for each ovary?

26. Sketch the pistil showing the seed-box or ovary, the stigma, and the style.

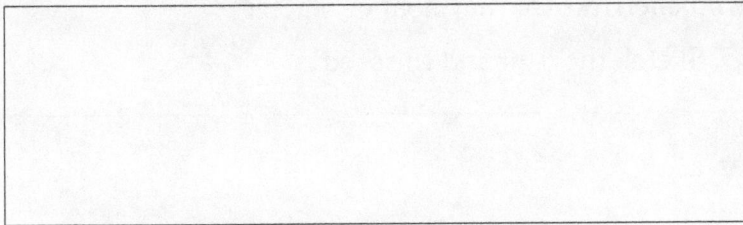

27. Is the blossom fragrant? Is there a nectary in the blossom? Watch the insects that visit the blossom and let them show you where the nectar is hidden.

28. What insects do you find visiting the flowers? Describe how they come into contact with the pollen and stigma, while they are seeking the nectar.

29. Do the flowers close during nights and dark stormy days? If they do not close, do they bend over? How do these movements protect the pollen?

30. How are the ripening seeds protected? Is each seed in a separate husk by itself? Is it with others in the pod-seed box or capsule? Are there many seeds together within one covering?

31. Describe the fruit.

....

....

....

....

....

....

32. By what means is the seed carried from its parent plant so that it may find a place to grow? Is it winged like the elms and maples? Has it a pappus balloon, like the milkweed and the dandelion? Does it attach itself to passers by, like the burs? Are the seeds blown out or are they shaken out by the wind as in the tulips and poppies? Are they thrown out like the seeds of witch hazel or jewelweed? Are They scattered by living creatures, as the squirrels carry acorns and nuts, and the birds berries and wild cherries? Do they float on water?

33. Sketch the fruit and the seed.

34. Is the plant beneficial or of any special importance to us? Is it beautiful? Is it a weed? Is it of use to animals or birds? If so, describe how.

Consult the manuals of plant and flower books and give an account of every thing that is of interest concerning this species, including its native place, its history and its uses by man; and any quotations from literature ---- especially poetry that may have been written concerning this species.

UNDERSCORE THE WORDS DESCRIBING THE PLANT.

1. Date

2. Name

3. Where is the plant found? In open field, hill-side, road-side, garden, woodland, swamp, brook-side, shore of pond or stream, in or on water?

4. How high does this plant grow?

5. Is the stem stiff, pliable, straight, drooping, twining, or creeping? Smooth, downy, rough, or thorny?

6. Is there a single stem or many coming from the same root? Is the stem branched? If the plant has a climbing habit, by what means does it cling to its support?

7. If the plant is a weed, or a cultivated plant, or very plentiful, study its roots. But if it is a beautiful wild flower, do not disturb it, as it is wrong thus to spoil our woods. Is the root fibrous or is it a tap root? Is it a storehouse for food?

8. Do you know whether the plant grows every year from the seed -- an annual, or does it live two years --a biannual; or does it grow year after year from the root -- a perennial?

9. Do the leaves grow at the base of the plant or along the stem? If along the stem, are they opposite or alternate? Is the leaf simple or compound?

10. Are the lower leaves of the same size and form as the upper leaves? Are the leaves polished, smooth, downy, hairy, or rough?

11. Sketch or trace a leaf, being careful to show its stem, veins, and especially to represent accurately the edges.

12. Where on the plant are the flowers borne? What is their general color?

13. Does each flower stand by itself or is it in a group with other flowers, if so, are the flowers arranged in a cluster or along the stem?

14. Which flowers blossom first, the nearest to the tip of the stem, or those nearest the base? In the case of the flowers that are in a cluster, do the outside or the center bloom first?

15. Study a single flower. Is its stem short or long, does it arise from the base of the plant or does it branch off of the stem of the plant? If the latter is the case, is there always a leaf where it comes off the stem?

16. Study the calyx or sepals. How many are there? Are they united?

17. Study the bud. Do the sepals protect the flower when it is in the bud? Do they protect the flower if it closes at night or during stormy days to protect its pollen?

18. Do the sepals fall off early as with the poppy, or do they remain after the seeds ripen? Do they protect the ripening seeds?

19. What color are the sepals? Do they always remain the same color or do they change color as with the lilies and tulips?

20. How many petals has the flower? How are they colored?

21. Sketch a single flower showing its sepals and petals, their form and arrangement.

22. Do you find stamens in the flower? If so, how many? Have they filaments or stems? Are they fastened to the petals? Are the filaments united at the bases as the hollyhock or geranium?

23. What is the color of the anthers? Is the anther attached at the middle or end to its stem, or filament? What color is the pollen? Can you see how the anther opens to let the pollen out?

24. Sketch a stamen showing the anther and filament.

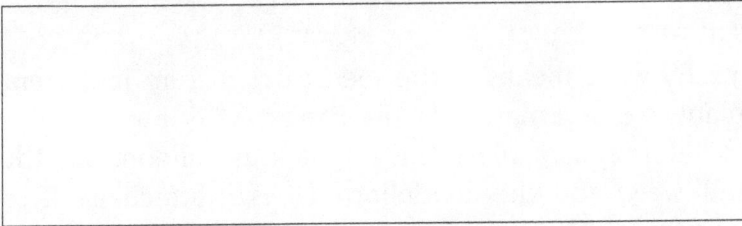

25. At the center of the flower find the pistil. Are there more than one, if so, how many? Is there a stem or style connecting the seed-box with its stigma? Is there more than one stigma for each ovary?

26. Sketch the pistil showing the seed-box or ovary, the stigma, and the style.

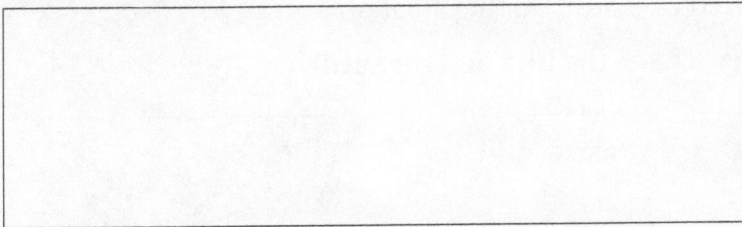

27. Is the blossom fragrant? Is there a nectary in the blossom? Watch the insects that visit the blossom and let them show you where the nectar is hidden.

28. What insects do you find visiting the flowers? Describe how they come into contact with the pollen and stigma, while they are seeking the nectar.

29. Do the flowers close during nights and dark stormy days? If they do not close, do they bend over? How do these movements protect the pollen?

30. How are the ripening seeds protected? Is each seed in a separate husk by itself? Is it with others in the pod-seed box or capsule? Are there many seeds together within one covering?

31. Describe the fruit.

....

....

....

....

....

....

32. By what means is the seed carried from its parent plant so that it may find a place to grow? Is it winged like the elms and maples? Has it a pappus balloon, like the milkweed and the dandelion? Does it attach itself to passers by, like the burs? Are the seeds blown out or are they shaken out by the wind as in the tulips and poppies? Are they thrown out like the seeds of witch hazel or jewelweed? Are They scattered by living creatures, as the squirrels carry acorns and nuts, and the birds berries and wild cherries? Do they float on water?

33. Sketch the fruit and the seed.

34. Is the plant beneficial or of any special importance to us? Is it beautiful? Is it a weed? Is it of use to animals or birds? If so, describe how.

Consult the manuals of plant and flower books and give an account of every thing that is of interest concerning this species, including its native place, its history and its uses by man; and any quotations from literature ---- especially poetry that may have been written concerning this species.

UNDERSCORE THE WORDS DESCRIBING THE PLANT.

1. Date

2. Name

3. Where is the plant found? In open field, hill-side, road-side, garden, woodland, swamp, brook-side, shore of pond or stream, in or on water?

4. How high does this plant grow?

5. Is the stem stiff, pliable, straight, drooping, twining, or creeping? Smooth, downy, rough, or thorny?

6. Is there a single stem or many coming from the same root? Is the stem branched? If the plant has a climbing habit, by what means does it cling to its support?

7. If the plant is a weed, or a cultivated plant, or very plentiful, study its roots. But if it is a beautiful wild flower, do not disturb it, as it is wrong thus to spoil our woods. Is the root fibrous or is it a tap root? Is it a storehouse for food?

8. Do you know whether the plant grows every year from the seed -- an annual, or does it live two years --a biannual; or does it grow year after year from the root -- a perennial?

9. Do the leaves grow at the base of the plant or along the stem? If along the stem, are they opposite or alternate? Is the leaf simple or compound?

10. Are the lower leaves of the same size and form as the upper leaves? Are the leaves polished, smooth, downy, hairy, or rough?

11. Sketch or trace a leaf, being careful to show its stem, veins, and especially to represent accurately the edges.

12. Where on the plant are the flowers borne? What is their general color?

13. Does each flower stand by itself or is it in a group with other flowers, if so, are the flowers arranged in a cluster or along the stem?

14. Which flowers blossom first, the nearest to the tip of the stem, or those nearest the base? In the case of the flowers that are in a cluster, do the outside or the center bloom first?

15. Study a single flower. Is its stem short or long, does it arise from the base of the plant or does it branch off of the stem of the plant? If the latter is the case, is there always a leaf where it comes off the stem?

16. Study the calyx or sepals. How many are there? Are they united?

17. Study the bud. Do the sepals protect the flower when it is in the bud? Do they protect the flower if it closes at night or during stormy days to protect its pollen?

18. Do the sepals fall off early as with the poppy, or do they remain after the seeds ripen? Do they protect the ripening seeds?

19. What color are the sepals? Do they always remain the same color or do they change color as with the lilies and tulips?

20. How many petals has the flower? How are they colored?

21. Sketch a single flower showing its sepals and petals, their form and arrangement.

22. Do you find stamens in the flower? If so, how many? Have they filaments or stems? Are they fastened to the petals? Are the filaments united at the bases as the hollyhock or geranium?

23. What is the color of the anthers? Is the anther attached at the middle or end to its stem, or filament? What color is the pollen? Can you see how the anther opens to let the pollen out?

24. Sketch a stamen showing the anther and filament.

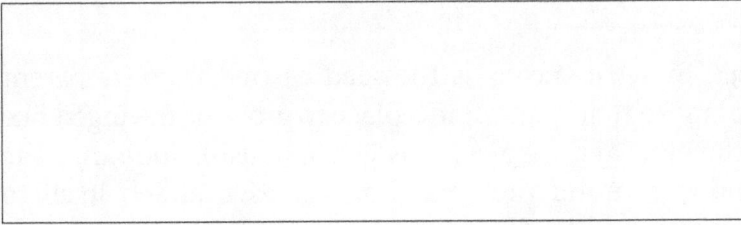

25. At the center of the flower find the pistil. Are there more than one, if so, how many? Is there a stem or style connecting the seed-box with its stigma? Is there more than one stigma for each ovary?

26. Sketch the pistil showing the seed-box or ovary, the stigma, and the style.

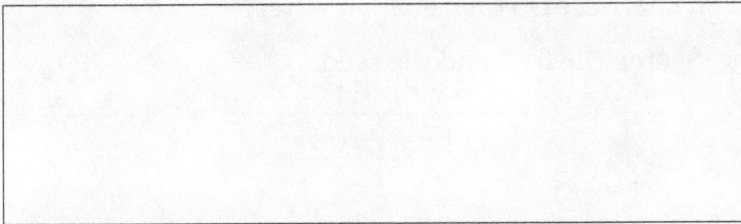

27. Is the blossom fragrant? Is there a nectary in the blossom? Watch the insects that visit the blossom and let them show you where the nectar is hidden.

28. What insects do you find visiting the flowers? Describe how they come into contact with the pollen and stigma, while they are seeking the nectar.

29. Do the flowers close during nights and dark stormy days? If they do not close, do they bend over? How do these movements protect the pollen?

30. How are the ripening seeds protected? Is each seed in a separate husk by itself? Is it with others in the pod-seed box or capsule? Are there many seeds together within one covering?

31. Describe the fruit.

....

....

....

....

....

....

32. By what means is the seed carried from its parent plant so that it may find a place to grow? Is it winged like the elms and maples? Has it a pappus balloon, like the milkweed and the dandelion? Does it attach itself to passers by, like the burs? Are the seeds blown out or are they shaken out by the wind as in the tulips and poppies? Are they thrown out like the seeds of witch hazel or jewelweed? Are They scattered by living creatures, as the squirrels carry acorns and nuts, and the birds berries and wild cherries? Do they float on water?

33. Sketch the fruit and the seed.

34. Is the plant beneficial or of any special importance to us? Is it beautiful? Is it a weed? Is it of use to animals or birds? If so, describe how.

Consult the manuals of plant and flower books and give an account of every thing that is of interest concerning this species, including its native place, its history and its uses by man; and any quotations from literature ---- especially poetry that may have been written concerning this species.

UNDERSCORE THE WORDS DESCRIBING THE PLANT.

1. Date

2. Name

3. Where is the plant found? In open field, hill-side, road-side, garden, woodland, swamp, brook-side, shore of pond or stream, in or on water?

4. How high does this plant grow?

5. Is the stem stiff, pliable, straight, drooping, twining, or creeping? Smooth, downy, rough, or thorny?

6. Is there a single stem or many coming from the same root? Is the stem branched? If the plant has a climbing habit, by what means does it cling to its support?

7. If the plant is a weed, or a cultivated plant, or very plentiful, study its roots. But if it is a beautiful wild flower, do not disturb it, as it is wrong thus to spoil our woods. Is the root fibrous or is it a tap root? Is it a storehouse for food?

8. Do you know whether the plant grows every year from the seed -- an annual, or does it live two years --a biannual; or does it grow year after year from the root -- a perennial?

9. Do the leaves grow at the base of the plant or along the stem? If along the stem, are they opposite or alternate? Is the leaf simple or compound?

10. Are the lower leaves of the same size and form as the upper leaves? Are the leaves polished, smooth, downy, hairy, or rough?

11. Sketch or trace a leaf, being careful to show its stem, veins, and especially to represent accurately the edges.

12. Where on the plant are the flowers borne? What is their general color?

13. Does each flower stand by itself or is it in a group with other flowers, if so, are the flowers arranged in a cluster or along the stem?

14. Which flowers blossom first, the nearest to the tip of the stem, or those nearest the base? In the case of the flowers that are in a cluster, do the outside or the center bloom first?

15. Study a single flower. Is its stem short or long, does it arise from the base of the plant or does it branch off of the stem of the plant? If the latter is the case, is there always a leaf where it comes off the stem?

16. Study the calyx or sepals. How many are there? Are they united?

17. Study the bud. Do the sepals protect the flower when it is in the bud? Do they protect the flower if it closes at night or during stormy days to protect its pollen?

18. Do the sepals fall off early as with the poppy, or do they remain after the seeds ripen? Do they protect the ripening seeds?

19. What color are the sepals? Do they always remain the same color or do they change color as with the lilies and tulips?

20. How many petals has the flower? How are they colored?

21. Sketch a single flower showing its sepals and petals, their form and arrangement.

22. Do you find stamens in the flower? If so, how many? Have they filaments or stems? Are they fastened to the petals? Are the filaments united at the bases as the hollyhock or geranium?

23. What is the color of the anthers? Is the anther attached at the middle or end to its stem, or filament? What color is the pollen? Can you see how the anther opens to let the pollen out?

24. Sketch a stamen showing the anther and filament.

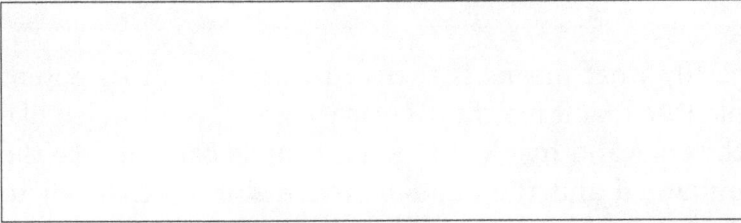

25. At the center of the flower find the pistil. Are there more than one, if so, how many? Is there a stem or style connecting the seed-box with its stigma? Is there more than one stigma for each ovary?

26. Sketch the pistil showing the seed-box or ovary, the stigma, and the style.

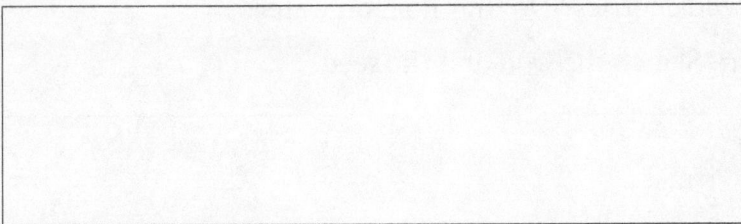

27. Is the blossom fragrant? Is there a nectary in the blossom? Watch the insects that visit the blossom and let them show you where the nectar is hidden.

28. What insects do you find visiting the flowers? Describe how they come into contact with the pollen and stigma, while they are seeking the nectar.

29. Do the flowers close during nights and dark stormy days? If they do not close, do they bend over? How do these movements protect the pollen?

30. How are the ripening seeds protected? Is each seed in a separate husk by itself? Is it with others in the pod-seed box or capsule? Are there many seeds together within one covering?

31. Describe the fruit.

....

....

....

....

....

....

32. By what means is the seed carried from its parent plant so that it may find a place to grow? Is it winged like the elms and maples? Has it a pappus balloon, like the milkweed and the dandelion? Does it attach itself to passers by, like the burs? Are the seeds blown out or are they shaken out by the wind as in the tulips and poppies? Are they thrown out like the seeds of witch hazel or jewelweed? Are They scattered by living creatures, as the squirrels carry acorns and nuts, and the birds berries and wild cherries? Do they float on water?

33. Sketch the fruit and the seed.

34. Is the plant beneficial or of any special importance to us? Is it beautiful? Is it a weed? Is it of use to animals or birds? If so, describe how.

Consult the manuals of plant and flower books and give an account of every thing that is of interest concerning this species, including its native place, its history and its uses by man; and any quotations from literature ---- especially poetry that may have been written concerning this species.

UNDERSCORE THE WORDS DESCRIBING THE PLANT.

1. Date

2. Name

3. Where is the plant found? In open field, hill-side, road-side, garden, woodland, swamp, brook-side, shore of pond or stream, in or on water?

4. How high does this plant grow?

5. Is the stem stiff, pliable, straight, drooping, twining, or creeping? Smooth, downy, rough, or thorny?

6. Is there a single stem or many coming from the same root? Is the stem branched? If the plant has a climbing habit, by what means does it cling to its support?

7. If the plant is a weed, or a cultivated plant, or very plentiful, study its roots. But if it is a beautiful wild flower, do not disturb it, as it is wrong thus to spoil our woods. Is the root fibrous or is it a tap root? Is it a storehouse for food?

8. Do you know whether the plant grows every year from the seed -- an annual, or does it live two years --a biannual; or does it grow year after year from the root -- a perennial?

9. Do the leaves grow at the base of the plant or along the stem? If along the stem, are they opposite or alternate? Is the leaf simple or compound?

10. Are the lower leaves of the same size and form as the upper leaves? Are the leaves polished, smooth, downy, hairy, or rough?

11. Sketch or trace a leaf, being careful to show its stem, veins, and especially to represent accurately the edges.

12. Where on the plant are the flowers borne? What is their general color?

13. Does each flower stand by itself or is it in a group with other flowers, if so, are the flowers arranged in a cluster or along the stem?

14. Which flowers blossom first, the nearest to the tip of the stem, or those nearest the base? In the case of the flowers that are in a cluster, do the outside or the center bloom first?

15. Study a single flower. Is its stem short or long, does it arise from the base of the plant or does it branch off of the stem of the plant? If the latter is the case, is there always a leaf where it comes off the stem?

16. Study the calyx or sepals. How many are there? Are they united?

17. Study the bud. Do the sepals protect the flower when it is in the bud? Do they protect the flower if it closes at night or during stormy days to protect its pollen?

18. Do the sepals fall off early as with the poppy, or do they remain after the seeds ripen? Do they protect the ripening seeds?

19. What color are the sepals? Do they always remain the same color or do they change color as with the lilies and tulips?

20. How many petals has the flower? How are they colored?

21. Sketch a single flower showing its sepals and petals, their form and arrangement.

22. Do you find stamens in the flower? If so, how many? Have they filaments or stems? Are they fastened to the petals? Are the filaments united at the bases as the hollyhock or geranium?

23. What is the color of the anthers? Is the anther attached at the middle or end to its stem, or filament? What color is the pollen? Can you see how the anther opens to let the pollen out?

24. Sketch a stamen showing the anther and filament.

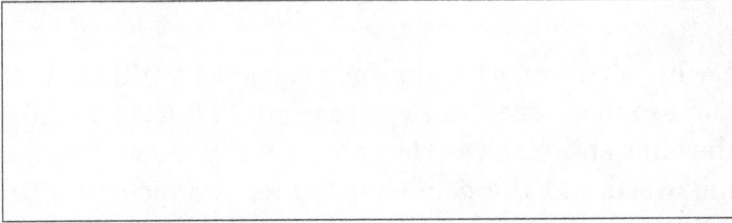

25. At the center of the flower find the pistil. Are there more than one, if so, how many? Is there a stem or style connecting the seed-box with its stigma? Is there more than one stigma for each ovary?

26. Sketch the pistil showing the seed-box or ovary, the stigma, and the style.

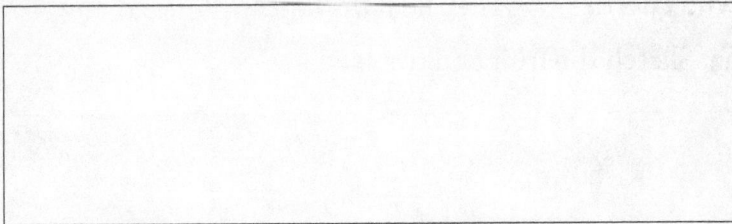

27. Is the blossom fragrant? Is there a nectary in the blossom? Watch the insects that visit the blossom and let them show you where the nectar is hidden.

28. What insects do you find visiting the flowers? Describe how they come into contact with the pollen and stigma, while they are seeking the nectar.

29. Do the flowers close during nights and dark stormy days? If they do not close, do they bend over? How do these movements protect the pollen?

30. How are the ripening seeds protected? Is each seed in a separate husk by itself? Is it with others in the pod-seed box or capsule? Are there many seeds together within one covering?

31. Describe the fruit.

....

....

....

....

....

....

32. By what means is the seed carried from its parent plant so that it may find a place to grow? Is it winged like the elms and maples? Has it a pappus balloon, like the milkweed and the dandelion? Does it attach itself to passers by, like the burs? Are the seeds blown out or are they shaken out by the wind as in the tulips and poppies? Are they thrown out like the seeds of witch hazel or jewelweed? Are They scattered by living creatures, as the squirrels carry acorns and nuts, and the birds berries and wild cherries? Do they float on water?

33. Sketch the fruit and the seed.

34. Is the plant beneficial or of any special importance to us? Is it beautiful? Is it a weed? Is it of use to animals or birds? If so, describe how.

Consult the manuals of plant and flower books and give an account of every thing that is of interest concerning this species, including its native place, its history and its uses by man; and any quotations from literature ---- especially poetry that may have been written concerning this species.

UNDERSCORE THE WORDS DESCRIBING THE PLANT.

1. Date

2. Name

3. Where is the plant found? In open field, hill-side, road-side, garden, woodland, swamp, brook-side, shore of pond or stream, in or on water?

4. How high does this plant grow?

5. Is the stem stiff, pliable, straight, drooping, twining, or creeping? Smooth, downy, rough, or thorny?

6. Is there a single stem or many coming from the same root? Is the stem branched? If the plant has a climbing habit, by what means does it cling to its support?

7. If the plant is a weed, or a cultivated plant, or very plentiful, study its roots. But if it is a beautiful wild flower, do not disturb it, as it is wrong thus to spoil our woods. Is the root fibrous or is it a tap root? Is it a storehouse for food?

8. Do you know whether the plant grows every year from the seed -- an annual, or does it live two years --a biannual; or does it grow year after year from the root -- a perennial?

9. Do the leaves grow at the base of the plant or along the stem? If along the stem, are they opposite or alternate? Is the leaf simple or compound?

10. Are the lower leaves of the same size and form as the upper leaves? Are the leaves polished, smooth, downy, hairy, or rough?

11. Sketch or trace a leaf, being careful to show its stem, veins, and especially to represent accurately the edges.

51

12. Where on the plant are the flowers borne? What is their general color?

13. Does each flower stand by itself or is it in a group with other flowers, if so, are the flowers arranged in a cluster or along the stem?

14. Which flowers blossom first, the nearest to the tip of the stem, or those nearest the base? In the case of the flowers that are in a cluster, do the outside or the center bloom first?

15. Study a single flower. Is its stem short or long, does it arise from the base of the plant or does it branch off of the stem of the plant? If the latter is the case, is there always a leaf where it comes off the stem?

16. Study the calyx or sepals. How many are there? Are they united?

17. Study the bud. Do the sepals protect the flower when it is in the bud? Do they protect the flower if it closes at night or during stormy days to protect its pollen?

18. Do the sepals fall off early as with the poppy, or do they remain after the seeds ripen? Do they protect the ripening seeds?

19. What color are the sepals? Do they always remain the same color or do they change color as with the lilies and tulips?

20. How many petals has the flower? How are they colored?

21. Sketch a single flower showing its sepals and petals, their form and arrangement.

22. Do you find stamens in the flower? If so, how many? Have they filaments or stems? Are they fastened to the petals? Are the filaments united at the bases as the hollyhock or geranium?

23. What is the color of the anthers? Is the anther attached at the middle or end to its stem, or filament? What color is the pollen? Can you see how the anther opens to let the pollen out?

24. Sketch a stamen showing the anther and filament.

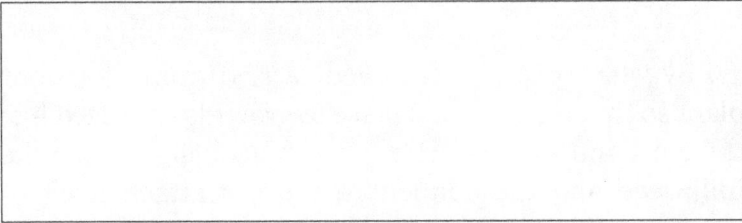

25. At the center of the flower find the pistil. Are there more than one, if so, how many? Is there a stem or style connecting the seed-box with its stigma? Is there more than one stigma for each ovary?

26. Sketch the pistil showing the seed-box or ovary, the stigma, and the style.

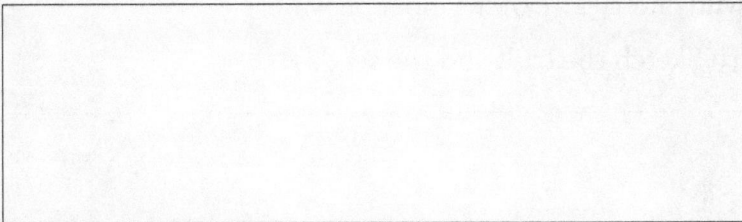

27. Is the blossom fragrant? Is there a nectary in the blossom? Watch the insects that visit the blossom and let them show you where the nectar is hidden.

28. What insects do you find visiting the flowers? Describe how they come into contact with the pollen and stigma, while they are seeking the nectar.

29. Do the flowers close during nights and dark stormy days? If they do not close, do they bend over? How do these movements protect the pollen?

30. How are the ripening seeds protected? Is each seed in a separate husk by itself? Is it with others in the pod-seed box or capsule? Are there many seeds together within one covering?

31. Describe the fruit.

....

....

....

....

....

....

32. By what means is the seed carried from its parent plant so that it may find a place to grow? Is it winged like the elms and maples? Has it a pappus balloon, like the milkweed and the dandelion? Does it attach itself to passers by, like the burs? Are the seeds blown out or are they shaken out by the wind as in the tulips and poppies? Are they thrown out like the seeds of witch hazel or jewelweed? Are They scattered by living creatures, as the squirrels carry acorns and nuts, and the birds berries and wild cherries? Do they float on water?

33. Sketch the fruit and the seed.

34. Is the plant beneficial or of any special importance to us? Is it beautiful? Is it a weed? Is it of use to animals or birds? If so, describe how.

Consult the manuals of plant and flower books and give an account of every thing that is of interest concerning this species, including its native place, its history and its uses by man; and any quotations from literature ---- especially poetry that may have been written concerning this species.

UNDERSCORE THE WORDS DESCRIBING THE PLANT.

1. Date

2. Name

3. Where is the plant found? In open field, hill-side, road-side, garden, woodland, swamp, brook-side, shore of pond or stream, in or on water?

4. How high does this plant grow?

5. Is the stem stiff, pliable, straight, drooping, twining, or creeping? Smooth, downy, rough, or thorny?

6. Is there a single stem or many coming from the same root? Is the stem branched? If the plant has a climbing habit, by what means does it cling to its support?

7. If the plant is a weed, or a cultivated plant, or very plentiful, study its roots. But if it is a beautiful wild flower, do not disturb it, as it is wrong thus to spoil our woods. Is the root fibrous or is it a tap root? Is it a storehouse for food?

8. Do you know whether the plant grows every year from the seed -- an annual, or does it live two years --a biannual; or does it grow year after year from the root -- a perennial?

9. Do the leaves grow at the base of the plant or along the stem? If along the stem, are they opposite or alternate? Is the leaf simple or compound?

10. Are the lower leaves of the same size and form as the upper leaves? Are the leaves polished, smooth, downy, hairy, or rough?

11. Sketch or trace a leaf, being careful to show its stem, veins, and especially to represent accurately the edges.

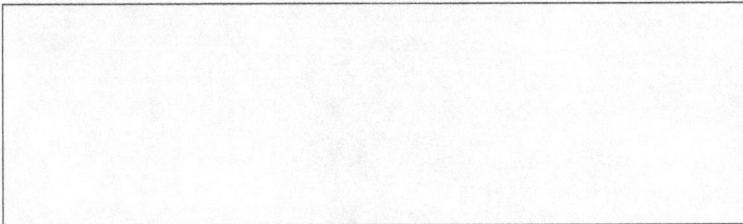

12. Where on the plant are the flowers borne? What is their general color?

13. Does each flower stand by itself or is it in a group with other flowers, if so, are the flowers arranged in a cluster or along the stem?

14. Which flowers blossom first, the nearest to the tip of the stem, or those nearest the base? In the case of the flowers that are in a cluster, do the outside or the center bloom first?

15. Study a single flower. Is its stem short or long, does it arise from the base of the plant or does it branch off of the stem of the plant? If the latter is the case, is there always a leaf where it comes off the stem?

16. Study the calyx or sepals. How many are there? Are they united?

17. Study the bud. Do the sepals protect the flower when it is in the bud? Do they protect the flower if it closes at night or during stormy days to protect its pollen?

18. Do the sepals fall off early as with the poppy, or do they remain after the seeds ripen? Do they protect the ripening seeds?

19. What color are the sepals? Do they always remain the same color or do they change color as with the lilies and tulips?

20. How many petals has the flower? How are they colored?

21. Sketch a single flower showing its sepals and petals, their form and arrangement.

22. Do you find stamens in the flower? If so, how many? Have they filaments or stems? Are they fastened to the petals? Are the filaments united at the bases as the hollyhock or geranium?

23. What is the color of the anthers? Is the anther attached at the middle or end to its stem, or filament? What color is the pollen? Can you see how the anther opens to let the pollen out?

24. Sketch a stamen showing the anther and filament.

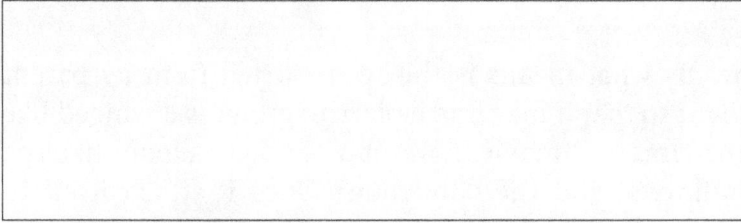

25. At the center of the flower find the pistil. Are there more than one, if so, how many? Is there a stem or style connecting the seed-box with its stigma? Is there more than one stigma for each ovary?

26. Sketch the pistil showing the seed-box or ovary, the stigma, and the style.

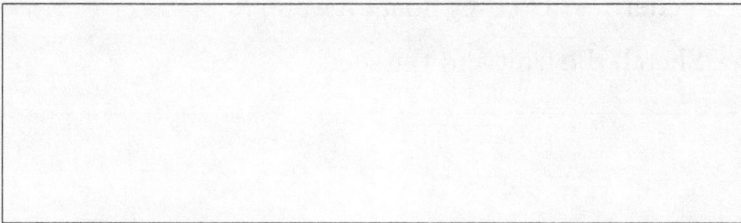

27. Is the blossom fragrant? Is there a nectary in the blossom? Watch the insects that visit the blossom and let them show you where the nectar is hidden.

28. What insects do you find visiting the flowers? Describe how they come into contact with the pollen and stigma, while they are seeking the nectar.

29. Do the flowers close during nights and dark stormy days? If they do not close, do they bend over? How do these movements protect the pollen?

30. How are the ripening seeds protected? Is each seed in a separate husk by itself? Is it with others in the pod-seed box or capsule? Are there many seeds together within one covering?

31. Describe the fruit.

....

....

....

....

....

....

32. By what means is the seed carried from its parent plant so that it may find a place to grow? Is it winged like the elms and maples? Has it a pappus balloon, like the milkweed and the dandelion? Does it attach itself to passers by, like the burs? Are the seeds blown out or are they shaken out by the wind as in the tulips and poppies? Are they thrown out like the seeds of witch hazel or jewelweed? Are They scattered by living creatures, as the squirrels carry acorns and nuts, and the birds berries and wild cherries? Do they float on water?

33. Sketch the fruit and the seed.

34. Is the plant beneficial or of any special importance to us? Is it beautiful? Is it a weed? Is it of use to animals or birds? If so, describe how.

Consult the manuals of plant and flower books and give an account of every thing that is of interest concerning this species, including its native place, its history and its uses by man; and any quotations from literature ---- especially poetry that may have been written concerning this species.

UNDERSCORE THE WORDS DESCRIBING THE PLANT.

1. Date

2. Name

3. Where is the plant found? In open field, hill-side, road-side, garden, woodland, swamp, brook-side, shore of pond or stream, in or on water?

4. How high does this plant grow?

5. Is the stem stiff, pliable, straight, drooping, twining, or creeping? Smooth, downy, rough, or thorny?

6. Is there a single stem or many coming from the same root? Is the stem branched? If the plant has a climbing habit, by what means does it cling to its support?

7. If the plant is a weed, or a cultivated plant, or very plentiful, study its roots. But if it is a beautiful wild flower, do not disturb it, as it is wrong thus to spoil our woods. Is the root fibrous or is it a tap root? Is it a storehouse for food?

8. Do you know whether the plant grows every year from the seed -- an annual, or does it live two years --a biannual; or does it grow year after year from the root -- a perennial?

9. Do the leaves grow at the base of the plant or along the stem? If along the stem, are they opposite or alternate? Is the leaf simple or compound?

10.Are the lower leaves of the same size and form as the upper leaves? Are the leaves polished, smooth, downy, hairy, or rough?

11. Sketch or trace a leaf, being careful to show its stem, veins, and especially to represent accurately the edges.

12. Where on the plant are the flowers borne? What is their general color?

13. Does each flower stand by itself or is it in a group with other flowers, if so, are the flowers arranged in a cluster or along the stem?

14. Which flowers blossom first, the nearest to the tip of the stem, or those nearest the base? In the case of the flowers that are in a cluster, do the outside or the center bloom first?

15. Study a single flower. Is its stem short or long, does it arise from the base of the plant or does it branch off of the stem of the plant? If the latter is the case, is there always a leaf where it comes off the stem?

16. Study the calyx or sepals. How many are there? Are they united?

17. Study the bud. Do the sepals protect the flower when it is in the bud? Do they protect the flower if it closes at night or during stormy days to protect its pollen?

18. Do the sepals fall off early as with the poppy, or do they remain after the seeds ripen? Do they protect the ripening seeds?

19. What color are the sepals? Do they always remain the same color or do they change color as with the lilies and tulips?

20. How many petals has the flower? How are they colored?

21. Sketch a single flower showing its sepals and petals, their form and arrangement.

22. Do you find stamens in the flower? If so, how many? Have they filaments or stems? Are they fastened to the petals? Are the filaments united at the bases as the hollyhock or geranium?

23. What is the color of the anthers? Is the anther attached at the middle or end to its stem, or filament? What color is the pollen? Can you see how the anther opens to let the pollen out?

24. Sketch a stamen showing the anther and filament.

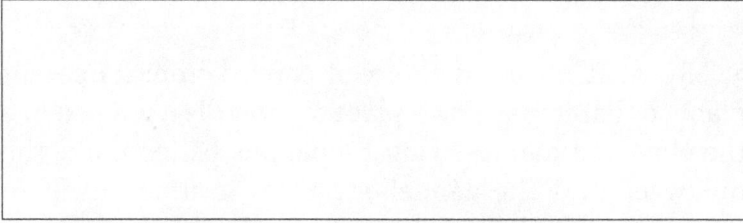

25. At the center of the flower find the pistil. Are there more than one, if so, how many? Is there a stem or style connecting the seed-box with its stigma? Is there more than one stigma for each ovary?

26. Sketch the pistil showing the seed-box or ovary, the stigma, and the style.

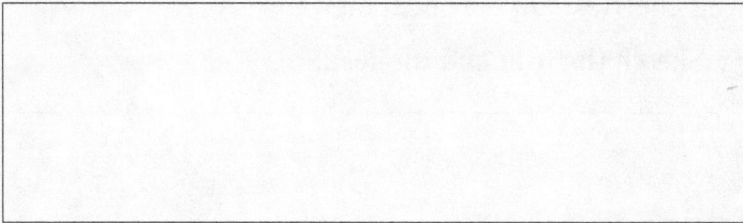

27. Is the blossom fragrant? Is there a nectary in the blossom? Watch the insects that visit the blossom and let them show you where the nectar is hidden.

28. What insects do you find visiting the flowers? Describe how they come into contact with the pollen and stigma, while they are seeking the nectar.

29. Do the flowers close during nights and dark stormy days? If they do not close, do they bend over? How do these movements protect the pollen?

30. How are the ripening seeds protected? Is each seed in a separate husk by itself? Is it with others in the pod-seed box or capsule? Are there many seeds together within one covering?

31. Describe the fruit.

....

....

....

....

....

....

32. By what means is the seed carried from its parent plant so that it may find a place to grow? Is it winged like the elms and maples? Has it a pappus balloon, like the milkweed and the dandelion? Does it attach itself to passers by, like the burs? Are the seeds blown out or are they shaken out by the wind as in the tulips and poppies? Are they thrown out like the seeds of witch hazel or jewelweed? Are They scattered by living creatures, as the squirrels carry acorns and nuts, and the birds berries and wild cherries? Do they float on water?

33. Sketch the fruit and the seed.

34. Is the plant beneficial or of any special importance to us? Is it beautiful? Is it a weed? Is it of use to animals or birds? If so, describe how.

Consult the manuals of plant and flower books and give an account of every thing that is of interest concerning this species, including its native place, its history and its uses by man; and any quotations from literature ---- especially poetry that may have been written concerning this species.

UNDERSCORE THE WORDS DESCRIBING THE PLANT.

1. Date

2. Name

3. Where is the plant found? In open field, hill-side, road-side, garden, woodland, swamp, brook-side, shore of pond or stream, in or on water?

4. How high does this plant grow?

5. Is the stem stiff, pliable, straight, drooping, twining, or creeping? Smooth, downy, rough, or thorny?

6. Is there a single stem or many coming from the same root? Is the stem branched? If the plant has a climbing habit, by what means does it cling to its support?

7. If the plant is a weed, or a cultivated plant, or very plentiful, study its roots. But if it is a beautiful wild flower, do not disturb it, as it is wrong thus to spoil our woods. Is the root fibrous or is it a tap root? Is it a storehouse for food?

8. Do you know whether the plant grows every year from the seed -- an annual, or does it live two years --a biannual; or does it grow year after year from the root -- a perennial?

9. Do the leaves grow at the base of the plant or along the stem? If along the stem, are they opposite or alternate? Is the leaf simple or compound?

10. Are the lower leaves of the same size and form as the upper leaves? Are the leaves polished, smooth, downy, hairy, or rough?

11. Sketch or trace a leaf, being careful to show its stem, veins, and especially to represent accurately the edges.

12. Where on the plant are the flowers borne? What is their general color?

13. Does each flower stand by itself or is it in a group with other flowers, if so, are the flowers arranged in a cluster or along the stem?

14. Which flowers blossom first, the nearest to the tip of the stem, or those nearest the base? In the case of the flowers that are in a cluster, do the outside or the center bloom first?

15. Study a single flower. Is its stem short or long, does it arise from the base of the plant or does it branch off of the stem of the plant? If the latter is the case, is there always a leaf where it comes off the stem?

16. Study the calyx or sepals. How many are there? Are they united?

17. Study the bud. Do the sepals protect the flower when it is in the bud? Do they protect the flower if it closes at night or during stormy days to protect its pollen?

18. Do the sepals fall off early as with the poppy, or do they remain after the seeds ripen? Do they protect the ripening seeds?

19. What color are the sepals? Do they always remain the same color or do they change color as with the lilies and tulips?

20. How many petals has the flower? How are they colored?

21. Sketch a single flower showing its sepals and petals, their form and arrangement.

22. Do you find stamens in the flower? If so, how many? Have they filaments or stems? Are they fastened to the petals? Are the filaments united at the bases as the hollyhock or geranium?

23. What is the color of the anthers? Is the anther attached at the middle or end to its stem, or filament? What color is the pollen? Can you see how the anther opens to let the pollen out?

24. Sketch a stamen showing the anther and filament.

25. At the center of the flower find the pistil. Are there more than one, if so, how many? Is there a stem or style connecting the seed-box with its stigma? Is there more than one stigma for each ovary?

26. Sketch the pistil showing the seed-box or ovary, the stigma, and the style.

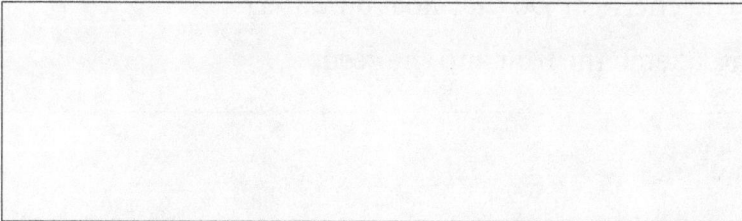

27. Is the blossom fragrant? Is there a nectary in the blossom? Watch the insects that visit the blossom and let them show you where the nectar is hidden.

28. What insects do you find visiting the flowers? Describe how they come into contact with the pollen and stigma, while they are seeking the nectar.

29. Do the flowers close during nights and dark stormy days? If they do not close, do they bend over? How do these movements protect the pollen?

30. How are the ripening seeds protected? Is each seed in a separate husk by itself? Is it with others in the pod-seed box or capsule? Are there many seeds together within one covering?

31. Describe the fruit.

....

....

....

....

....

....

32. By what means is the seed carried from its parent plant so that it may find a place to grow? Is it winged like the elms and maples? Has it a pappus balloon, like the milkweed and the dandelion? Does it attach itself to passers by, like the burs? Are the seeds blown out or are they shaken out by the wind as in the tulips and poppies? Are they thrown out like the seeds of witch hazel or jewelweed? Are They scattered by living creatures, as the squirrels carry acorns and nuts, and the birds berries and wild cherries? Do they float on water?

33. Sketch the fruit and the seed.

34. Is the plant beneficial or of any special importance to us? Is it beautiful? Is it a weed? Is it of use to animals or birds? If so, describe how.

Consult the manuals of plant and flower books and give an account of every thing that is of interest concerning this species, including its native place, its history and its uses by man; and any quotations from literature ---- especially poetry that may have been written concerning this species.

UNDERSCORE THE WORDS DESCRIBING THE PLANT.

1. Date

2. Name

3. Where is the plant found? In open field, hill-side, road-side, garden, woodland, swamp, brook-side, shore of pond or stream, in or on water?

4. How high does this plant grow?

5. Is the stem stiff, pliable, straight, drooping, twining, or creeping? Smooth, downy, rough, or thorny?

6. Is there a single stem or many coming from the same root? Is the stem branched? If the plant has a climbing habit, by what means does it cling to its support?

7. If the plant is a weed, or a cultivated plant, or very plentiful, study its roots. But if it is a beautiful wild flower, do not disturb it, as it is wrong thus to spoil our woods. Is the root fibrous or is it a tap root? Is it a storehouse for food?

8. Do you know whether the plant grows every year from the seed -- an annual, or does it live two years --a biannual; or does it grow year after year from the root -- a perennial?

9. Do the leaves grow at the base of the plant or along the stem? If along the stem, are they opposite or alternate? Is the leaf simple or compound?

10. Are the lower leaves of the same size and form as the upper leaves? Are the leaves polished, smooth, downy, hairy, or rough?

11. Sketch or trace a leaf, being careful to show its stem, veins, and especially to represent accurately the edges.

12. Where on the plant are the flowers borne? What is their general color?

13. Does each flower stand by itself or is it in a group with other flowers, if so, are the flowers arranged in a cluster or along the stem?

14. Which flowers blossom first, the nearest to the tip of the stem, or those nearest the base? In the case of the flowers that are in a cluster, do the outside or the center bloom first?

15. Study a single flower. Is its stem short or long, does it arise from the base of the plant or does it branch off of the stem of the plant? If the latter is the case, is there always a leaf where it comes off the stem?

16. Study the calyx or sepals. How many are there? Are they united?

17. Study the bud. Do the sepals protect the flower when it is in the bud? Do they protect the flower if it closes at night or during stormy days to protect its pollen?

18. Do the sepals fall off early as with the poppy, or do they remain after the seeds ripen? Do they protect the ripening seeds?

19. What color are the sepals? Do they always remain the same color or do they change color as with the lilies and tulips?

20. How many petals has the flower? How are they colored?

21. Sketch a single flower showing its sepals and petals, their form and arrangement.

22. Do you find stamens in the flower? If so, how many? Have they filaments or stems? Are they fastened to the petals? Are the filaments united at the bases as the hollyhock or geranium?

23. What is the color of the anthers? Is the anther attached at the middle or end to its stem, or filament? What color is the pollen? Can you see how the anther opens to let the pollen out?

24. Sketch a stamen showing the anther and filament.

25. At the center of the flower find the pistil. Are there more than one, if so, how many? Is there a stem or style connecting the seed-box with its stigma? Is there more than one stigma for each ovary?

26. Sketch the pistil showing the seed-box or ovary, the stigma, and the style.

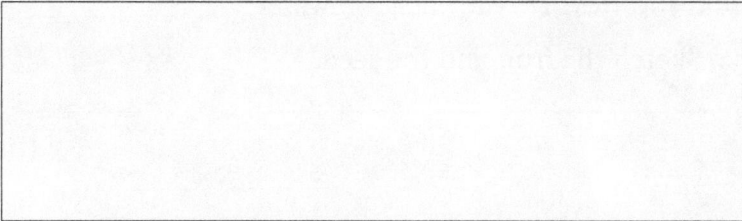

27. Is the blossom fragrant? Is there a nectary in the blossom? Watch the insects that visit the blossom and let them show you where the nectar is hidden.

28. What insects do you find visiting the flowers? Describe how they come into contact with the pollen and stigma, while they are seeking the nectar.

29. Do the flowers close during nights and dark stormy days? If they do not close, do they bend over? How do these movements protect the pollen?

30. How are the ripening seeds protected? Is each seed in a separate husk by itself? Is it with others in the pod-seed box or capsule? Are there many seeds together within one covering?

31. Describe the fruit.

....

....

....

....

....

....

32. By what means is the seed carried from its parent plant so that it may find a place to grow? Is it winged like the elms and maples? Has it a pappus balloon, like the milkweed and the dandelion? Does it attach itself to passers by, like the burs? Are the seeds blown out or are they shaken out by the wind as in the tulips and poppies? Are they thrown out like the seeds of witch hazel or jewelweed? Are They scattered by living creatures, as the squirrels carry acorns and nuts, and the birds berries and wild cherries? Do they float on water?

33. Sketch the fruit and the seed.

34. Is the plant beneficial or of any special importance to us? Is it beautiful? Is it a weed? Is it of use to animals or birds? If so, describe how.

Consult the manuals of plant and flower books and give an account of every thing that is of interest concerning this species, including its native place, its history and its uses by man; and any quotations from literature ---- especially poetry that may have been written concerning this species.

UNDERSCORE THE WORDS DESCRIBING THE PLANT.

1. Date

2. Name

3. Where is the plant found? In open field, hill-side, road-side, garden, woodland, swamp, brook-side, shore of pond or stream, in or on water?

4. How high does this plant grow?

5. Is the stem stiff, pliable, straight, drooping, twining, or creeping? Smooth, downy, rough, or thorny?

6. Is there a single stem or many coming from the same root? Is the stem branched? If the plant has a climbing habit, by what means does it cling to its support?

7. If the plant is a weed, or a cultivated plant, or very plentiful, study its roots. But if it is a beautiful wild flower, do not disturb it, as it is wrong thus to spoil our woods. Is the root fibrous or is it a tap root? Is it a storehouse for food?

8. Do you know whether the plant grows every year from the seed -- an annual, or does it live two years --a biannual; or does it grow year after year from the root -- a perennial?

9. Do the leaves grow at the base of the plant or along the stem? If along the stem, are they opposite or alternate? Is the leaf simple or compound?

10. Are the lower leaves of the same size and form as the upper leaves? Are the leaves polished, smooth, downy, hairy, or rough?

11. Sketch or trace a leaf, being careful to show its stem, veins, and especially to represent accurately the edges.

12. Where on the plant are the flowers borne? What is their general color?

13. Does each flower stand by itself or is it in a group with other flowers, if so, are the flowers arranged in a cluster or along the stem?

14. Which flowers blossom first, the nearest to the tip of the stem, or those nearest the base? In the case of the flowers that are in a cluster, do the outside or the center bloom first?

15. Study a single flower. Is its stem short or long, does it arise from the base of the plant or does it branch off of the stem of the plant? If the latter is the case, is there always a leaf where it comes off the stem?

16. Study the calyx or sepals. How many are there? Are they united?

17. Study the bud. Do the sepals protect the flower when it is in the bud? Do they protect the flower if it closes at night or during stormy days to protect its pollen?

18. Do the sepals fall off early as with the poppy, or do they remain after the seeds ripen? Do they protect the ripening seeds?

19. What color are the sepals? Do they always remain the same color or do they change color as with the lilies and tulips?

20. How many petals has the flower? How are they colored?

21. Sketch a single flower showing its sepals and petals, their form and arrangement.

22. Do you find stamens in the flower? If so, how many? Have they filaments or stems? Are they fastened to the petals? Are the filaments united at the bases as the hollyhock or geranium?

23. What is the color of the anthers? Is the anther attached at the middle or end to its stem, or filament? What color is the pollen? Can you see how the anther opens to let the pollen out?

24. Sketch a stamen showing the anther and filament.

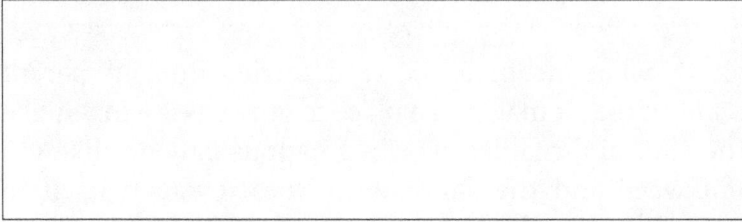

25. At the center of the flower find the pistil. Are there more than one, if so, how many? Is there a stem or style connecting the seed-box with its stigma? Is there more than one stigma for each ovary?

26. Sketch the pistil showing the seed-box or ovary, the stigma, and the style.

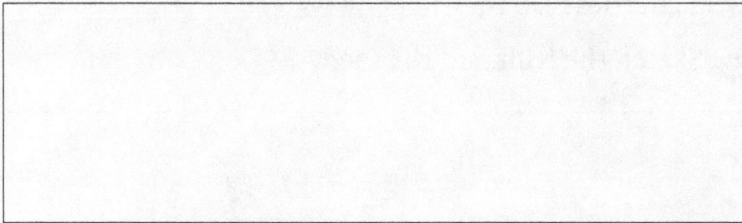

27. Is the blossom fragrant? Is there a nectary in the blossom? Watch the insects that visit the blossom and let them show you where the nectar is hidden.

28. What insects do you find visiting the flowers? Describe how they come into contact with the pollen and stigma, while they are seeking the nectar.

29. Do the flowers close during nights and dark stormy days? If they do not close, do they bend over? How do these movements protect the pollen?

30. How are the ripening seeds protected? Is each seed in a separate husk by itself? Is it with others in the pod-seed box or capsule? Are there many seeds together within one covering?

31. Describe the fruit.

....

....

....

....

....

....

32. By what means is the seed carried from its parent plant so that it may find a place to grow? Is it winged like the elms and maples? Has it a pappus balloon, like the milkweed and the dandelion? Does it attach itself to passers by, like the burs? Are the seeds blown out or are they shaken out by the wind as in the tulips and poppies? Are they thrown out like the seeds of witch hazel or jewelweed? Are They scattered by living creatures, as the squirrels carry acorns and nuts, and the birds berries and wild cherries? Do they float on water?

33. Sketch the fruit and the seed.

34. Is the plant beneficial or of any special importance to us? Is it beautiful? Is it a weed? Is it of use to animals or birds? If so, describe how.

Consult the manuals of plant and flower books and give an account of every thing that is of interest concerning this species, including its native place, its history and its uses by man; and any quotations from literature ---- especially poetry that may have been written concerning this species.

UNDERSCORE THE WORDS DESCRIBING THE PLANT.

1. Date

2. Name

3. Where is the plant found? In open field, hill-side, road-side, garden, woodland, swamp, brook-side, shore of pond or stream, in or on water?

4. How high does this plant grow?

5. Is the stem stiff, pliable, straight, drooping, twining, or creeping? Smooth, downy, rough, or thorny?

6. Is there a single stem or many coming from the same root? Is the stem branched? If the plant has a climbing habit, by what means does it cling to its support?

7. If the plant is a weed, or a cultivated plant, or very plentiful, study its roots. But if it is a beautiful wild flower, do not disturb it, as it is wrong thus to spoil our woods. Is the root fibrous or is it a tap root? Is it a storehouse for food?

8. Do you know whether the plant grows every year from the seed -- an annual, or does it live two years --a biannual; or does it grow year after year from the root -- a perennial?

9. Do the leaves grow at the base of the plant or along the stem? If along the stem, are they opposite or alternate? Is the leaf simple or compound?

10. Are the lower leaves of the same size and form as the upper leaves? Are the leaves polished, smooth, downy, hairy, or rough?

11. Sketch or trace a leaf, being careful to show its stem, veins, and especially to represent accurately the edges.

12. Where on the plant are the flowers borne? What is their general color?

13. Does each flower stand by itself or is it in a group with other flowers, if so, are the flowers arranged in a cluster or along the stem?

14. Which flowers blossom first, the nearest to the tip of the stem, or those nearest the base? In the case of the flowers that are in a cluster, do the outside or the center bloom first?

15. Study a single flower. Is its stem short or long, does it arise from the base of the plant or does it branch off of the stem of the plant? If the latter is the case, is there always a leaf where it comes off the stem?

16. Study the calyx or sepals. How many are there? Are they united?

17. Study the bud. Do the sepals protect the flower when it is in the bud? Do they protect the flower if it closes at night or during stormy days to protect its pollen?

18. Do the sepals fall off early as with the poppy, or do they remain after the seeds ripen? Do they protect the ripening seeds?

19. What color are the sepals? Do they always remain the same color or do they change color as with the lilies and tulips?

20. How many petals has the flower? How are they colored?

21. Sketch a single flower showing its sepals and petals, their form and arrangement.

22. Do you find stamens in the flower? If so, how many? Have they filaments or stems? Are they fastened to the petals? Are the filaments united at the bases as the hollyhock or geranium?

23. What is the color of the anthers? Is the anther attached at the middle or end to its stem, or filament? What color is the pollen? Can you see how the anther opens to let the pollen out?

24. Sketch a stamen showing the anther and filament.

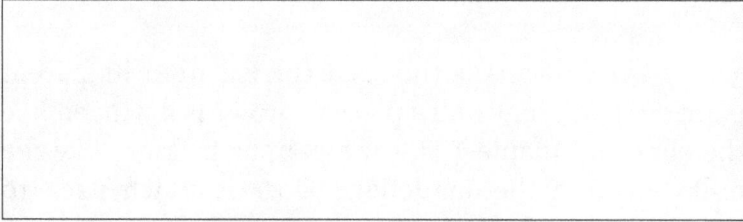

25. At the center of the flower find the pistil. Are there more than one, if so, how many? Is there a stem or style connecting the seed-box with its stigma? Is there more than one stigma for each ovary?

26. Sketch the pistil showing the seed-box or ovary, the stigma, and the style.

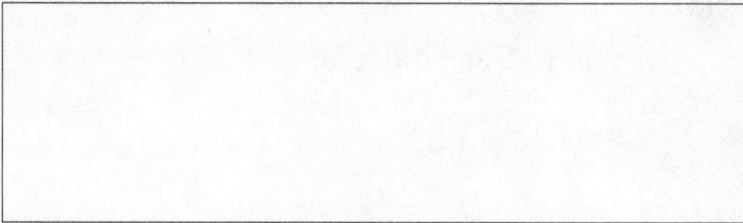

27. Is the blossom fragrant? Is there a nectary in the blossom? Watch the insects that visit the blossom and let them show you where the nectar is hidden.

28. What insects do you find visiting the flowers? Describe how they come into contact with the pollen and stigma, while they are seeking the nectar.

29. Do the flowers close during nights and dark stormy days? If they do not close, do they bend over? How do these movements protect the pollen?

30. How are the ripening seeds protected? Is each seed in a separate husk by itself? Is it with others in the pod-seed box or capsule? Are there many seeds together within one covering?

31. Describe the fruit.

....

....

....

....

....

....

32. By what means is the seed carried from its parent plant so that it may find a place to grow? Is it winged like the elms and maples? Has it a pappus balloon, like the milkweed and the dandelion? Does it attach itself to passers by, like the burs? Are the seeds blown out or are they shaken out by the wind as in the tulips and poppies? Are they thrown out like the seeds of witch hazel or jewelweed? Are They scattered by living creatures, as the squirrels carry acorns and nuts, and the birds berries and wild cherries? Do they float on water?

33. Sketch the fruit and the seed.

34. Is the plant beneficial or of any special importance to us? Is it beautiful? Is it a weed? Is it of use to animals or birds? If so, describe how.

Consult the manuals of plant and flower books and give an account of every thing that is of interest concerning this species, including its native place, its history and its uses by man; and any quotations from literature ---- especially poetry that may have been written concerning this species.

UNDERSCORE THE WORDS DESCRIBING THE PLANT.

1. Date

2. Name

3. Where is the plant found? In open field, hill-side, road-side, garden, woodland, swamp, brook-side, shore of pond or stream, in or on water?

4. How high does this plant grow?

5. Is the stem stiff, pliable, straight, drooping, twining, or creeping? Smooth, downy, rough, or thorny?

6. Is there a single stem or many coming from the same root? Is the stem branched? If the plant has a climbing habit, by what means does it cling to its support?

7. If the plant is a weed, or a cultivated plant, or very plentiful, study its roots. But if it is a beautiful wild flower, do not disturb it, as it is wrong thus to spoil our woods. Is the root fibrous or is it a tap root? Is it a storehouse for food?

8. Do you know whether the plant grows every year from the seed -- an annual, or does it live two years --a biannual; or does it grow year after year from the root -- a perennial?

9. Do the leaves grow at the base of the plant or along the stem? If along the stem, are they opposite or alternate? Is the leaf simple or compound?

10. Are the lower leaves of the same size and form as the upper leaves? Are the leaves polished, smooth, downy, hairy, or rough?

11. Sketch or trace a leaf, being careful to show its stem, veins, and especially to represent accurately the edges.

12. Where on the plant are the flowers borne? What is their general color?

13. Does each flower stand by itself or is it in a group with other flowers, if so, are the flowers arranged in a cluster or along the stem?

14. Which flowers blossom first, the nearest to the tip of the stem, or those nearest the base? In the case of the flowers that are in a cluster, do the outside or the center bloom first?

15. Study a single flower. Is its stem short or long, does it arise from the base of the plant or does it branch off of the stem of the plant? If the latter is the case, is there always a leaf where it comes off the stem?

16. Study the calyx or sepals. How many are there? Are they united?

17. Study the bud. Do the sepals protect the flower when it is in the bud? Do they protect the flower if it closes at night or during stormy days to protect its pollen?

18. Do the sepals fall off early as with the poppy, or do they remain after the seeds ripen? Do they protect the ripening seeds?

19. What color are the sepals? Do they always remain the same color or do they change color as with the lilies and tulips?

20. How many petals has the flower? How are they colored?

21. Sketch a single flower showing its sepals and petals, their form and arrangement.

22. Do you find stamens in the flower? If so, how many? Have they filaments or stems? Are they fastened to the petals? Are the filaments united at the bases as the hollyhock or geranium?

23. What is the color of the anthers? Is the anther attached at the middle or end to its stem, or filament? What color is the pollen? Can you see how the anther opens to let the pollen out?

24. Sketch a stamen showing the anther and filament.

25. At the center of the flower find the pistil. Are there more than one, if so, how many? Is there a stem or style connecting the seed-box with its stigma? Is there more than one stigma for each ovary?

26. Sketch the pistil showing the seed-box or ovary, the stigma, and the style.

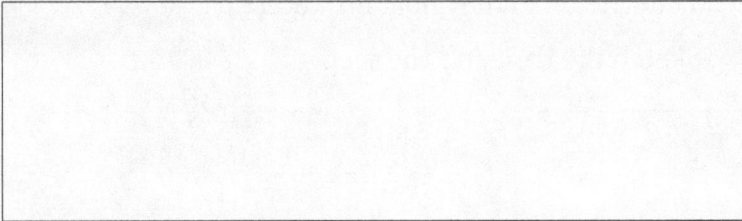

27. Is the blossom fragrant? Is there a nectary in the blossom? Watch the insects that visit the blossom and let them show you where the nectar is hidden.

28. What insects do you find visiting the flowers? Describe how they come into contact with the pollen and stigma, while they are seeking the nectar.

29. Do the flowers close during nights and dark stormy days? If they do not close, do they bend over? How do these movements protect the pollen?

30. How are the ripening seeds protected? Is each seed in a separate husk by itself? Is it with others in the pod-seed box or capsule? Are there many seeds together within one covering?

31. Describe the fruit.

....

....

....

....

....

....

32. By what means is the seed carried from its parent plant so that it may find a place to grow? Is it winged like the elms and maples? Has it a pappus balloon, like the milkweed and the dandelion? Does it attach itself to passers by, like the burs? Are the seeds blown out or are they shaken out by the wind as in the tulips and poppies? Are they thrown out like the seeds of witch hazel or jewelweed? Are They scattered by living creatures, as the squirrels carry acorns and nuts, and the birds berries and wild cherries? Do they float on water?

33. Sketch the fruit and the seed.

34. Is the plant beneficial or of any special importance to us? Is it beautiful? Is it a weed? Is it of use to animals or birds? If so, describe how.

Consult the manuals of plant and flower books and give an account of every thing that is of interest concerning this species, including its native place, its history and its uses by man; and any quotations from literature ---- especially poetry that may have been written concerning this species.

PLANTS WITH COMPOSITE FLOWERS

The sunflower, daisy, goldenrod, aster, black-eyed Susan, thistle, dandelion, life everlasting, burdock, chicory, tansy, dahlia, chrysanthemum, marigold, bachelor's button, barguerite, zinnia, cosmos and many others.

If a single flower of a geranium, verbana, or clover plants were to stand alone by itself it would attract little attention from insects; but with several or many of these flowers grouped together in a natural bouquet they form a showy mass that is attractive to insects' eyes as well as to ours.

There is one order of plants that has gone farther than this and have their flowers grouped into little families, each member of the family doing its part of the work. Those flowers at the center are small and inconspicuous but produce the pollen, seed and nectar; while those members of the family situated on the outside have banners usually of white or yellow that are very showy and attract the attention of insects to the whole family. The daisy, aster, dandelion, goldenrod, and many others have their flowers thus arranged. The thistles and burdocks and some others do not have conspicuous banner flowers.

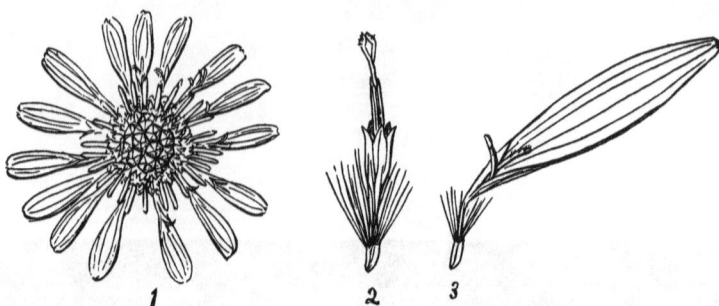

1   2   3

This family arrangement of the flowers is rather difficult for us to understand because those flowers which carry the banners look like the petals of an ordinary flower; but, if carefully examined, we can see that each is a single flower. The little flower in the center, or the "disk flower" as it is called, is a tubular flower with a five-pointed corolla and instead of having separate stamens, the anthers take hold of hands and form a tube through which the stigma pushes out all of the pollen and then opens up in Y-shape to receive pollen from some other flower.

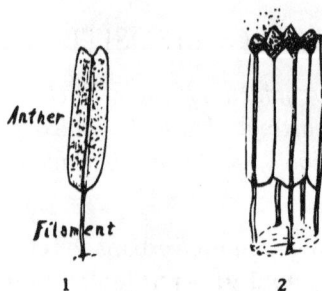

Anther

Filament

1   2

Each of these little flower families live on top of a little green house made of bracts, which is called the involucre. These bracts do the same work for the flower family that the sepals do for an ordinary flower; they protect the whole family, when in bud, and also, in some cases like those of the asters and dandelion, close up around the family in dark weather and nights, and also protect the developing seeds.

Each little flower of such a flower family is called a floret, which means, "little flower." Those with banners are called the banner - or ray-florets, those at the center are called the disk-florets. In the sunflower the banner-florets do not develop any seed, but in the daisies, asters, and others, each banner-floret has a seed and a stigma. The disk-florets all develop seeds and also develop pollen in their anther tubes.

The study of the composites should begin with the large sunflower. Take one that is just opening, place its stem in water and watch it for a week, noticing just what happens and how many of the florets blossom each day. Around the edge of the disk the banner florets flare wide, they have long petals like the rays of the sun; of the disk florets those on the outside blossom first and those at the very center may blossom a week later. After the study of the great sunflower it will be easy to see and understand the flowers of the asters, the goldenrod, and the daisies.

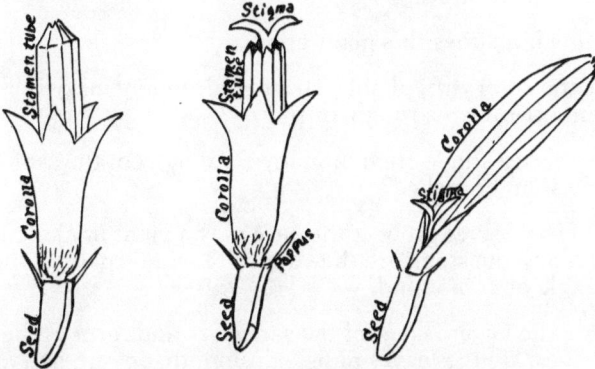

Disk floret in early stage.   *Disk floret in later stage.*   *Banner or ray floret.*

Each little flower of such a flower family is called a floret, which means, "little flower." Those with banners are called the banner - or ray-florets, those at the center are called the disk-florets. In the sunflower the banner-florets do not develop any seed, but in the daisies, asters, and others, each banner-floret has a seed and a stigma. The disk-florets all develop seeds and also develop pollen in their anther tubes.

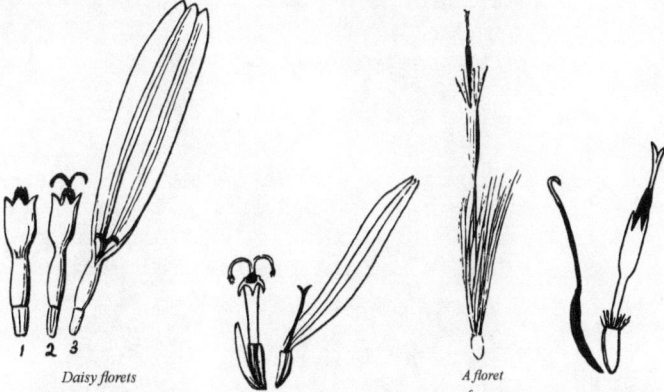

Daisy florets
1. Disk-flower in pollen stage;
2. Disk-flower in stigma stage;
3. Ray-flower.   All enlarged.

Disk-flower and ray-flower of black-eyed Susan.

A floret from a thistle flower-head

A burdock floret with hooked bract

Plants with Composite Flowers

1. Date

2. Name

3. Where is the plant found? In open field, hill-side, road-side, the garden, woodland, swamps, brook-side, shore of pond or stream, or on water?

4. How high does this plant grow?

5. Is the stem stiff, pliable, straight, drooping, or twining, smooth, downy, rough, or thorny?

6. Is there a single stem or many coming from the same root; is the stem branched?

7. Do the leaves grow at the base of the plant or along the stem; if along the stem, are they opposite or alternate; is the leaf single or compound?

8. Are the lower leaves of the same size and form as the upper leaves; are the leaves polished, smooth, downy, hairy, or rough?

9. Sketch or trace a leaf, being careful to show its stem, veins, and especially, to represent accurately its edges.

10. Is there one flower family at the top of the stem, as in the daisies, or are there many set along the stem like the goldenrod?

11. What color are the disk-florets?

12. What color are the banner-florets?

13. How many banner-florets to a family?

14. Is there a stigma in the banner-floret, and is a seed developed below it?

15. How many disk-florets are there or are there too many to count?

16. Sketch the flower family roughly showing the banners extending out around the   disk.

17. Describe the involucre or "green house" on which the family lives: are the bracts smooth, downy, hairy or spiny?

18. Sketch one of the bracts:

19. Do the bracts close up around the family during the night and stormy weather?

20. Do the bracts close up around the family after the florets have blossomed?

21. Sketch a seed and describe how it is carried away from the mother plant, so that it may find room to grow.

22. Is the plant beneficial or of any special importance to us? Is it beautiful? Is it a weed? Is it of use to animals or birds? If so, describe how.

PLANTS WITH COMPOSITE FLOWERS

1. Date

2. Name

3. Where is the plant found? In open field, hill-side, road-side, the garden, woodland, swamps, brook-side, shore of pond or stream, or on water?

4. How high does this plant grow?

5. Is the stem stiff, pliable, straight, drooping, or twining, smooth, downy, rough, or thorny?

6. Is there a single stem or many coming from the same root; is the stem branched?

7. Do the leaves grow at the base of the plant or along the stem; if along the stem, are they opposite or alternate; is the leaf single or compound?

8. Are the lower leaves of the same size and form as the upper leaves; are the leaves polished, smooth, downy, hairy, or rough?

9. Sketch or trace a leaf, being careful to show its stem, veins, and especially, to represent accurately its edges.

10. Is there one flower family at the top of the stem, as in the daisies, or are there many set along the stem like the goldenrod?

11. What color are the disk-florets?

12. What color are the banner-florets?

13. How many banner-florets to a family?

14. Is there a stigma in the banner-floret, and is a seed developed below it?

15. How many disk-florets are there or are there too many to count?

16. Sketch the flower family roughly showing the banners extending out around the   disk.

17. Describe the involucre or "green house" on which the family lives: are the bracts smooth, downy, hairy or spiny?

18. Sketch one of the bracts:

19. Do the bracts close up around the family during the night and stormy weather?

20. Do the bracts close up around the family after the florets have blossomed?

21. Sketch a seed and describe how it is carried away from the mother plant, so that it may find room to grow.

22. Is the plant beneficial or of any special importance to us? Is it beautiful? Is it a weed? Is it of use to animals or birds? If so, describe how.

PLANTS WITH COMPOSITE FLOWERS

1. Date

2. Name

3. Where is the plant found? In open field, hill-side, road-side, the garden, woodland, swamps, brook-side, shore of pond or stream, or on water?

4. How high does this plant grow?

5. Is the stem stiff, pliable, straight, drooping, or twining, smooth, downy, rough, or thorny?

6. Is there a single stem or many coming from the same root; is the stem branched?

7. Do the leaves grow at the base of the plant or along the stem; if along the stem, are they opposite or alternate; is the leaf single or compound?

8. Are the lower leaves of the same size and form as the upper leaves; are the leaves polished, smooth, downy, hairy, or rough?

9. Sketch or trace a leaf, being careful to show its stem, veins, and especially, to represent accurately its edges.

10. Is there one flower family at the top of the stem, as in the daisies, or are there many set along the stem like the goldenrod?

11. What color are the disk-florets?

12. What color are the banner-florets?

13. How many banner-florets to a family?

14. Is there a stigma in the banner-floret, and is a seed developed below it?

15. How many disk-florets are there or are there too many to count?

16. Sketch the flower family roughly showing the banners extending out around the   disk.

17. Describe the involucre or "green house" on which the family lives: are the bracts smooth, downy, hairy or spiny?

18. Sketch one of the bracts:

19. Do the bracts close up around the family during the night and stormy weather?

20. Do the bracts close up around the family after the florets have blossomed?

21. Sketch a seed and describe how it is carried away from the mother plant, so that it may find room to grow.

22. Is the plant beneficial or of any special importance to us? Is it beautiful? Is it a weed? Is it of use to animals or birds? If so, describe how.

PLANTS WITH COMPOSITE FLOWERS

1. Date

2. Name

3. Where is the plant found? In open field, hill-side, road-side, the garden, woodland, swamps, brook-side, shore of pond or stream, or on water?

4. How high does this plant grow?

5. Is the stem stiff, pliable, straight, drooping, or twining, smooth, downy, rough, or thorny?

6. Is there a single stem or many coming from the same root; is the stem branched?

7. Do the leaves grow at the base of the plant or along the stem; if along the stem, are they opposite or alternate; is the leaf single or compound?

8. Are the lower leaves of the same size and form as the upper leaves; are the leaves polished, smooth, downy, hairy, or rough?

9. Sketch or trace a leaf, being careful to show its stem, veins, and especially, to represent accurately its edges.

10. Is there one flower family at the top of the stem, as in the daisies, or are there many set along the stem like the goldenrod?

11. What color are the disk-florets?

12. What color are the banner-florets?

13. How many banner-florets to a family?

14. Is there a stigma in the banner-floret, and is a seed developed below it?

15. How many disk-florets are there or are there too many to count?

16. Sketch the flower family roughly showing the banners extending out around the   disk.

17. Describe the involucre or "green house" on which the family lives: are the bracts smooth, downy, hairy or spiny?

18. Sketch one of the bracts:

19. Do the bracts close up around the family during the night and stormy weather?

20. Do the bracts close up around the family after the florets have blossomed?

21. Sketch a seed and describe how it is carried away from the mother plant, so that it may find room to grow.

22. Is the plant beneficial or of any special importance to us? Is it beautiful? Is it a weed? Is it of use to animals or birds? If so, describe how.

PLANTS WITH COMPOSITE FLOWERS

1. Date

2. Name

3. Where is the plant found? In open field, hill-side, road-side, the garden, woodland, swamps, brook-side, shore of pond or stream, or on water?

4. How high does this plant grow?

5. Is the stem stiff, pliable, straight, drooping, or twining, smooth, downy, rough, or thorny?

6. Is there a single stem or many coming from the same root; is the stem branched?

7. Do the leaves grow at the base of the plant or along the stem; if along the stem, are they opposite or alternate; is the leaf single or compound?

8. Are the lower leaves of the same size and form as the upper leaves; are the leaves polished, smooth, downy, hairy, or rough?

9. Sketch or trace a leaf, being careful to show its stem, veins, and especially, to represent accurately its edges.

10. Is there one flower family at the top of the stem, as in the daisies, or are there many set along the stem like the goldenrod?

11. What color are the disk-florets?

12. What color are the banner-florets?

13. How many banner-florets to a family?

14. Is there a stigma in the banner-floret, and is a seed developed below it?

15. How many disk-florets are there or are there too many to count?

16. Sketch the flower family roughly showing the banners extending out around the   disk.

17. Describe the involucre or "green house" on which the family lives: are the bracts smooth, downy, hairy or spiny?

18. Sketch one of the bracts:

19. Do the bracts close up around the family during the night and stormy weather?

20. Do the bracts close up around the family after the florets have blossomed?

21. Sketch a seed and describe how it is carried away from the mother plant, so that it may find room to grow.

22. Is the plant beneficial or of any special importance to us? Is it beautiful? Is it a weed? Is it of use to animals or birds? If so, describe how.

WILD FLOWER KEY

MEADOW BEAUTY   EVENING PRIMROSE   WILD SARSAPARILLA   WATER PARSNIP

PRINCE'S PINE   SHIN-LEAF   ONE-FLOWERED PYROLA   INDIAN PIPE

ARBUTUS   FOUR-LEAVED LOOSESTRIFE   SHOOTING STAR   MONEYWORT

SPREADING DOGBANE   COMMON MILKWEED   MORNING GLORY   DOWNY PELOX

SKULLCAP   CATNIP   GROUND IVY   SELF-HEAL   MOTHERWORT

WILD CARROT FLOWERING DOGWOOD BUNCHBERRY SPOTTED WINTERGREEN

FALSE
BEECH DROPS PINK AZALEA MOUNTAIN LAUREL WINTERGREEN

   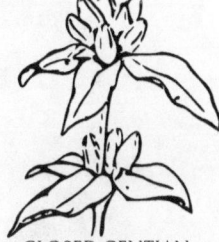

STAR FLOWER PIMPERNEL FRINGED GENTIAN CLOSED GENTIAN

MOSS PINK FORGET-ME-NOT VIPER'S BUGLOSS BLUE VERVAIN

OSWEGO TEA SPEARMINT PEPPERMINT WILD MINT

CAT-TAIL ARROW-HEAD JACK-IN-THE-PULPIT WATER ARUM

PICKEREL-WEED MUD PLANTAIN BELLWORT BELLWORT

ADDERS TONGUE CLINTONIA WILD SPIKENARD CANADA MAYFLOWER

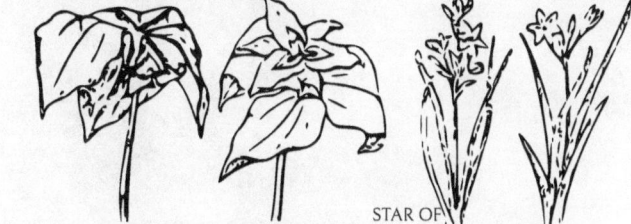

STAR OF
NODDING TRILLIUM PAINTED TRILLIUM BETHLEHEM STAR GRASS

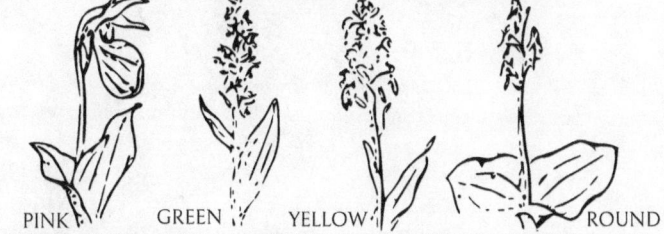

PINK GREEN YELLOW ROUND
LADY'S SLIPPER FRINGED ORCHIS FRINGED ORCHIS LEAVED ORCHIS

GOLDEN CLUB SKUNK CABBAGE DAY-FLOWER SPIDERWORT

DAY LILY WOOD LILY TURK'S CAP LILY CANADA LILY

SOLOMON'S SEAL INDIAN CUCUMBER-ROOT PURPLE TRILLIUM WHITE TRILLIUM

BLUE IRIS BLUE-EYED GRASS YELLOW LADY'S SLIPPER SHOWY LADY'S SLIPPER

GRASS PINK INDIAN PINK SNAKE MOUTH NODDING POGONIA WHORLED POGONIA SHOWY ORCHIS

131

RATTLE
SNAKE PLANTAIN   LADIES' TRESSES   TWAYSLADE   WILD GINGER

BLADDER CAMPION BOUNCING BET SPRING BEAUTY   WATER LILY

WOOD ANEMONE RUE ANEMONE PURPLE CLEMATIS WHITE CLEMATIS

MANDRAKE   BLOODROOT   ALANDINE   DUTCHMAN'S BREECHES

SUNDOWN   GRASS-OF-PARNASSUS   EARLY SAXIFRAGE   MITREWORT

LADY'S THUMB   SMARTWEED   TEARTHUMB   CORN COCKLE   RAGGED ROBIN

YELLOW POND LILY   MARSH MARIGOLD   BUTTERCUP   MEADOW RUE

WILD COLUMBINE   GOLDTHREAD   MONKSHOOD   HEPATICA

SQUIRREL CORN   TOOTHWORT   COMMON MUSTARD   PITCHER PLANT

FOAM FLOWER   HARDHACK   MEADOWSWEET   WILD STRAWBERRY   COMMON CINQUEFOIL

PURPLE
CINQUEFOIL

AGRIMONY

CREEPING DALIBARDA

YELLOW AVENS

SWEETBRIAR ROSE

WILD INDIGO

BLUE LUPINE

PARTRIDGE PEA

YELLOW SWEET CLOVER

ALFALFA

BLUE VETCH

GROUND NUT

WILD GERANIUM

HERB ROBERT

FRINGED POLYGALA

FIELD MILKWORT

COMMON ST JOHNS WORT

FROSTWEED

BIRD-FOOT VIOLET

PALMATED VIOLET

BARREN STRAWBERRY   PURPLE FLOWERING RASPBERRY   PASTURE ROSE

RABBIT FOOT CLOVER   RED CLOVER   ALSIKE CLOVER WHITE CLOVER HOP CLOVER

WHITE   YELLOW

HOG PEANUT   TICK TREFOIL   COMMON FLAX WOOD SORREL   WOOD SORREL

JEWEL-WEED   COMMON MALLOW   MUSK MALLOW   ROSE MALLOW

LANCED   DOWNY

COMMON VIOLET   SWEET WHITE VIOLET   LEAVED VIOLET   YELLOW VIOLET

BITTERSWEET

JIMSON WEED

GREAT MULLEIN

MOTH MULLEIN

INDIAN PAINT BRUSH

WOOD BETONY

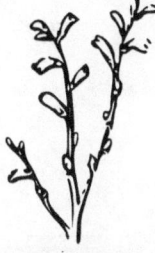
BEECH DROPS

BROOM-RAPE

HAREBELL

CADINAL FLOWER

JOE PYE WEED

BONE SET

ELECAMPANE

PURPLE
CONE FLOWER

BLACK-EYED SUSAN

BUR-MARIGOLD

TANSY

BURDOCK

CANADA THISTLE

BULL THISTLE

TOADPLAY   TURTLE-HEAD   MONKEY FLOWER   FOX GLOVE

BLUETS   PARTRIDGEBERRY   TWIN FLOWER   TEASEL   BELLFLOWER

GOLDENROD   ASTER   ROBIN'S PLAINTAIN   PUSSY'S TOES   PEARL EVERLASTING

DAISY   FEVERFEW   VARROW   MAYWEED   SNEEZEWEED

CHICORY   DANDELION   HAWKWEED

www.ingramcontent.com/pod-product-compliance
Lightning Source LLC
Chambersburg PA
CBHW022059020426
42335CB00012B/748